Killin' Generals

Killin' Generals

The Making of
The Dirty Dozen,
the Most Iconic WWII Movie
of All Time

DWAYNE EPSTEIN

Citadel Press
Kensington Publishing Corp.
www.kensingtonbooks.com

CITADEL PRESS BOOKS are published by

Kensington Publishing Corp.
119 West 40th Street
New York, NY 10018

Copyright © 2023 by Dwayne Epstein

All rights reserved. No part of this book may be reproduced in any form or by any means without the prior written consent of the publisher, excepting brief quotes used in reviews.

All Kensington titles, imprints, and distributed lines are available at special quantity discounts for bulk purchases for sales promotions, premiums, fund-raising, educational, or institutional use. Special book excerpts or customized printings can also be created to fit specific needs. For details, write or phone the office of the Kensington sales manager: Kensington Publishing Corp., 119 West 40th Street, New York, NY 10018, attn: Sales Department; phone 1-800-221-2647.

CITADEL PRESS and the Citadel logo are Reg. U.S. Pat. & TM Off.

ISBN: 978-0-8065-4241-6

First Citadel hardcover printing: May 2023

10 9 8 7 6 5 4 3 2 1

Printed in the United States of America

Library of Congress Control Number: 2022950825

ISBN: 978-0-8065-4243-0 (e-book)

For Mike, he knows why;
and to Barbara, she knows why

CONTENTS

INTRODUCTION

A TALE OF REDEMPTION

It was perfect. I was twelve, thirteen years old; going through puberty. Here was this totally macho, rock 'em–sock 'em, heroic action movie—one of the best 'mission' movies ever made. Everything about it, top to bottom, was cool. And it turned me on to the movies. In a lot of ways, it made me want to go to the movies every single week to try to have that kind of experience that would just take you away.
—OSCAR-WINNING DIRECTOR RON HOWARD

1967 saw the release of such recognized classics as *Bonnie and Clyde, The Graduate, Guess Who's Coming to Dinner, Cool Hand Luke*, and *In the Heat of the Night*. All these titles were groundbreaking classics. However, the film Ron Howard was referring to was one of the biggest box office successes of the year, *The Dirty Dozen*.

The two-and-a-half-hour film is set during World War II, when renegade Major John Reisman (Lee Marvin) is assigned to train twelve military prisoners convicted of violent crimes for a suicide mission behind enemy lines. The film is structured in three parts: the recruitment of prisoners, their training, and the climactic mission. The result is an influential classic that still resonates more than fifty years later. The point of *Killin' Generals* is to explore the film's inception, production, reception, and lasting legacy.

Accomplishing this is no easy task, but through the use of archival materials, memos, long-out-of-print books, and periodicals, it will be attempted herein. Highlights of the research include new and exclusive interviews with participants, such as producer Ken Hyman; actors Donald Sutherland, Dora Reisser, and Colin Maitland; and a rare, unpublished interview with author E. M. Nathanson, on whose novel the film is based. Also speaking candidly about the film are surviving family members of Clint Walker, Robert Ryan, and others. Exclusive interviews conducted during research for *Lee Marvin: Point Blank* concerning *The Dirty Dozen* were not included in that book but are prevalent in this narrative.

Many myths have been created about *The Dirty Dozen*, such as its basis in reality, what cast members actually thought of it, and who was meant to star in it and why. There are still ongoing controversies surrounding the film and the reasons for its popularity. Was it anti-war? Antiestablishment? Anti-authority? Its brutal ending shocked audiences and critics at the time of its release, and although the world has changed, it still packs a wallop to this day. The scene showing the incineration of perceived innocent civilians is still debated among movie enthusiasts.

The film's star, WWII combat veteran Lee Marvin, defended it at the time, stating, "Life is a violent situation. Let's not kid ourselves about that. It's not just the men in the chalet who were Nazis; the women were part of it too. I liked the idea of the final scene because it was their job to destroy the whole group, and maybe in some way speed the demise of the Third Reich. We glorify the Eighth Air Force for bombing cities when they killed one hundred thousand in one night, but remember, there were a lot of women and children burned up in those raids."

Whether one agrees with that assessment or not, there is still an undeniable appeal to the film that echoes through the decades. The nonconformity of the title characters aside, the theme that redemption of even the worst of humanity can still be achieved, or, at the very least, honestly attempted, underpins the film. It's what drove the novel's author, E. M. Nathanson, to write the tale. When done believably, with healthy doses of appropriate or bawdy humor, you have something akin to *The Dirty Dozen*. Created before the advent of CGI, the realistic pyrotechnic action exploding onscreen kept the film memorable.

The film has been able to resonate through the decades in many ways. In the 1993 romantic comedy *Sleepless in Seattle*, Tom Hanks and Victor Garber tease Rita Wilson and Rosie O'Donnell when they cry as they talk about the ending of *An Affair to Remember* (1957). The men respond by shedding fake tears over *The Dirty Dozen*, especially Richard Jaeckel's helmet.

The website for the popular cable network Turner Classic Movies (TCM), which frequently airs the film, cites several pop culture references, including the use of the title of the film in the name of the popular New Orleans jazz group the Dirty Dozen Brass Band. The term "dirty dozen" is now in fairly widespread use, generally referring to a group of undesirables, such as the twelve most-contaminated types of produce or the IRS's list of the most common tax scams. The National Recreation and Park Association also uses the term for the twelve most common playground safety concerns, and the League of

Conservation Voters groups members of Congress who consistently vote against environmental causes under that title. A book published by the Cato Institute, a libertarian think tank, examining the twelve so-called worst Supreme Court cases from the authors' point of view is called *The Dirty Dozen: How Twelve Supreme Court Cases Radically Expanded Government and Eroded Freedom.*

Most of all, in its style, attitude, and pushing the envelope of violence, *The Dirty Dozen*, as TCM notes, can be seen as a major precursor to modern-day action films, particularly those that feature a group of unlikely heroes banding together for an impossible mission.

Released at a time of extreme nonconformity, Robert Aldrich's *Dirty Dozen* became popular with viewers of all age groups, no matter their point of view, whether pacifist or militarist. The final nose thumb of the film's last line—"Boy, oh boy. Killin' generals could get to be a habit with me"—was the ultimate Bronx cheer. It was delivered sarcastically by actor Charles Bronson at the film's finale after his character has witnessed the hypocrisy of his superiors. Redemption, loyalty, hypocrisy, competition, brutality, antiauthoritarianism, and nonconformity all played a role in making *The Dirty Dozen* the classic it has remained.

PART I

Inception

1

"THE HACKLES ON THE BACK OF MY NECK WENT UP"

Forcing a hulking giant to confront his suppressed homicidal temper, his rebellious commanding officer gives the man a knife and then goads him with taunts that will ultimately lead to a violent explosion.

The haunting image described above is from the pen of author E. M. Nathanson in his bestselling novel *The Dirty Dozen*. The unique tale of *The Dirty Dozen* had an equally unique origin. Born on February 17, 1928, in the Bronx, Erwin Michael Nathanson had a childhood he described as also worthy of a book. His parents split when he was young due to his mother's clinical depression, forcing her to be institutionalized when the boy was only two. His father had to place his son in a Jewish orphanage in Manhattan until he was seven. He then went to the Hebrew National Orphan Home in Yonkers, where he stayed until he graduated high school.

Nathanson, known as Mick to his friends and family, passed away in 2016 at the age of eighty-eight. However, in

7

2006 in an unpublished interview with writer Beverly Gray, he
said, "When I was at the boy's home in Yonkers—I was about
eleven, maybe—I started working on the home newspaper.
That was my first writing. I still have some of those little articles. . . . Yeah, yeah, I'm still very close to some of the boys."

Despite having spent it in an orphanage, Nathanson
recalled, "It was a wonderful childhood." As he remembered
it, "We had a farm, twenty acres. We kids worked on the farm.
We planted and weeded and sowed and reaped. We grew our
own. It was terrific. . . . I liked being able to grow on the farm;
picked fresh vegetables and cantaloupes. We would go up to
the field where the cantaloupes were planted. In the later afternoon, we had the activity of going swimming somewhere. We
had a creek nearby. We'd call it 'BA.' People would ask what
that stands for, and we'd say 'Boys' Athletics' but actually it
was 'Bare-Assed.' We'd go into the fields afterward, just pick
some ripe cantaloupes and pop them open, lean against a tree,
and it's never tasted better since."

While at the orphanage he not only developed an interest
in writing but was influenced by the films he saw on Wednesday nights in the gymnasium: "We had a projector in the New
Gymnasium, as we called it. A screen would drop [down] from
the high ceiling. There was a projection room [at] one end. Just
like in a movie theater. People in the area would come and join
us, people that lived in that part of Yonkers, Tuckahoe. It was
a Wednesday night event.

"We also went out. We were permitted—invited, I suppose, by theater owners in Tuckahoe and nearby villages—to
go to the movies. Some of them were dramas and comedies.
What was very popular was the Errol Flynn–type of movies,
with the swords dangling from the yardarm and all that . . .

the next day we'd make these wooden swords and we'd be running through the halls of the orphan home."

After graduating high school, Nathanson enrolled in NYU's Washington Square College in Greenwich Village, where he majored in anthropology. However, he also had a job. "I had a full-time job that had started out as a part-time job before I went into the army," Nathanson recalled. "I worked for Fairchild Publications. Remember *Women's Wear Daily?* The *Daily News Record?* I was on the copy desk. I was a copy editor and rewrite man. I was only seventeen. I talked myself into the job. I started as a copy boy. Then maybe a year or less later, I got a copy of a book called *Headlines and Deadlines* by Robert E. Garst, the author, and Theodore Menline Bernstein, editor, who were prominent in the business. I read it and thought, *I know what to do.* So I went to the boss of the copy desk and I asked him for a job. He said okay. . . . I think I worked on the copy desk maybe a year before I went into the army."

When it came to his writing style, he learned by experience: "I worked as an associate editor of magazines at Fawcett Publications," he recalled. "True-crime magazines . . . and particularly what we used to call the 'dick' books, detective magazines. I learned to write there because before my writing was journalism, reporting, and very little feature work. These magazines were all features. I would come across one version of an old story in which a woman was wearing a brown coat and a new version saying she was wearing a blue coat. I would go to my boss, the editor of the magazine, 'This is wrong,' and he'd say, 'What's the difference? Just tell a good story. That's all.' So I learned how to take facts and turn them into good, exciting stories, and how to write dialogue. I mean, I didn't write these stories, although I did do a lot of rewriting of the stories. They were written by freelance writers.

"Occasionally I would get an opportunity to write one myself, in which case I made extra money. It was in the pulp magazine business that I learned to write, how to characterize, how to describe, and how to evoke a scene. I would try to create an exciting narrative with dialogue that may or may not have ever happened, but in context it seemed to me the dialogue probably took place.

I remember reading about a couple of guys from Germany or Austria, I think, who were on a round-the-world motorcycle trip. I got in touch with them and asked if they'd give me the story. They'd get the byline. I did two; one was about their adventures with some savage tribe and the other, I think, was about elephants. I got about three hundred dollars, and their byline got them at least one hundred dollars. So, I learned to write. I learned to take facts and descriptions and evoke the scene and make the characters vivid for the magazine readers. It really was a wonderful school."

He was fortunate enough to be called up toward the end of the war, serving roughly from 1946 to 1947. As he jokingly remembered, "Yeah, nobody was shooting at me, except there were people who wanted to. But they were on my side, theoretically."

He later gave more detail by explaining, "I went in, the war was over. I was eighteen. I had been in college for a while, working in college. I tried to enlist in the navy and changed my mind at the last moment. I wanted to finish the term at college. I knew I was going to go into the army soon, anyhow. So, I went in, in the spring of 1946 and I was out in the spring of 1947. One year was all it was. I was in the tail end of the drafting army, and Congress had cut the funds for the AUS, the Army of the United States, rather than the US Army, and they were trying to get rid of people to wait and walk home and stuff like that. It was costing them money.

"I was on a shipment to Germany and they asked me if I wanted to reenlist. They bumped my rank. I looked at my shoulders and arms, [*laughs*] 'What are you gonna bump?' I just said, 'No, I'll think about it.' I went home, which was then NYC, for the weekend. I talked to a couple of friends, people I had worked with on newspapers who had been in. A couple of them had been in and got shot up badly and got out, barely. They said, 'Get out! If they give you a chance to get out, get out!' So I said, 'Yeah, I think you're right. There are things that I wanted to do. I don't really want to stay in the army.' I came back and said, 'No, thank you. When you discharge me, I'll be discharged.'"

Ultimately, he chose to leave the service and took advantage of the GI Bill to go back to college. He never earned a degree, deciding instead to return to his writing career. The clerical experience he acquired in the army also led to something else that would serve him well in later years: "I didn't see combat when I was in the army. I was aware of it. Talked to people, buddies and friends from my childhood, who had been in by the time I got in. And people I worked with."

One of those friends would become central to Nathanson's creation of *The Dirty Dozen*. "I think they might have met in the army and [reconnected] in the later 1950s," recalled Nathanson's son, Michael. "I'm not one-hundred-percent sure of these details. They did become friends, and I remember as a child going to Russ Meyer's house with my parents occasionally, for a friendly poker game gathering and socializing."

The Russ Meyer he speaks of is the same sexploitation pioneer known for the popular films he made in the 1960s and '70s starring buxom women. Naturally, he didn't start out as Hollywood's "King Leer." Meyer was born March 21, 1922, near Oakland, California, and like Nathanson had parents who split up shortly after he was born. When he was fourteen, his mother pawned her wedding ring to buy her son an 8mm camera, beginning a lifelong film obsession with international repercussions.

Meyer's photographic prowess served him well during WWII, as he was assigned to the 166th Signal Photographic Company as a staff sergeant commissioned to the Third Army under George Patton. Some of the footage he filmed was later used in the film *Patton* (1970). Sometime in May 1944, Meyer received an assignment from Colonel Kirke B. Lawton that would become the stuff of legend.

After the war ended in 1945, Meyer pursued a career in Hollywood. His friend Mick Nathanson was in New York freelancing for the *Washington Post* and some true-crime, pulp, and detective magazines to earn a decent living and to support his bride, Mary Ann, and their young son, Michael. During the early 1950s, he recalled being in a bar on Forty-Second Street chatting with a struggling young actor: "It was a theater bar where we closed that bar one night. He was discussing whether or not to stay in Hollywood or come back to New York. He'd had some success in TV at that point and he didn't know what to do with himself. I was the last person to advise him. I knew absolutely nothing." The struggling young actor was Lee Marvin.

Nathanson was facing the same challenge in terms of his future, not sure if he should stay in New York or go to California. Ultimately, he chose California, where, among other things, he reunited with his friend Russ Meyer. In fact, Meyer had set up production on his first "nudie cutie" entitled *The Immoral Mr. Teas* (1959). Meyer cowrote, directed, and produced the rather innocuous little film about a traveling salesman who sees beautiful nude women wherever he goes. Meyer filmed it with several of his friends from his army days, including Bill Teas as the title character and Mick Nathanson, credited as assistant director. He can also be seen onscreen as an audience member during the burlesque show sequence.

That same year, probably during a poker game, Meyer and Nathanson had a casual conversation about what Nathanson was currently working on. The writer said that he had just come back from San Diego, where he had been working with a naval officer on a story about a really fouled-up squadron of WWII aviators. Meyer then said, "Oh, that reminds me of the Dirty Dozen." Intrigued, Nathanson wanted to hear more about it.

At a stockade near Southampton, England, Meyer had been assigned to film a dozen US Army prisoners who had been convicted of such capital crimes as murder, rape, or, in some cases, both, and were therefore sentenced to death. They were told their sentences might be commuted if they agreed to parachute behind enemy lines before D-Day on a top-secret sabotage mission. Meyer filmed them training for about forty minutes, noting that one was Native American and another was African American, but all were unshaven and unkempt. When Meyer asked why they looked so disheveled, an MP told him they had been uncooperative and refused to bathe or shave.

Meyer sent his two hundred feet of film to headquarters. After D-Day, he inquired with his superiors about the whereabouts of the dozen and was told they had successfully parachuted to their mission but hadn't been heard from since.

Hearing the tale, Nathanson later told his friend Frank McAdams, "The hackles on the back of my neck went up. I was excited by the dramatic possibilities of these men in that situation." Nathanson wanted to hear more about the men as the genesis of an exclusive nonfiction novel began to take shape in his mind. He continued to pepper Meyer with questions; as Nathanson recalled, "Russ told me where the film went when it left his camera. It crossed the desk of a major in England, Major Fox—he was related to the Fox family—and that guy responded to a letter. He remembered it but he didn't know anything more about it. Other people said, 'Oh yeah. I remember a group like that.'"

With Meyer's help, Nathanson began researching in earnest. According to his son Michael, "I remember him saying that the mission was never fully executed because the D-Day invasion became a reality, and all efforts and resources were focused there.

"My father had the naturally inquisitive mind of a reporter. His curiosity was piqued, and he did enormous amounts of research, combing through the National Archives and other sources to prepare to develop the idea of *The Dirty Dozen*. If I remember correctly, he really began in earnest shortly after he returned, sick as a dog with pneumonia, from covering the 1960 Winter Olympics at Squaw Valley for some piece he was doing."

Undeterred by his illness, Nathanson continued to search for any evidence of Meyer's Dirty Dozen and their mission. As a journalist and a veteran, he had access to such resources as the Pentagon Library and the National Archives. Discovering tidbits of information that would often lead to dead ends, he began rethinking his concept of a nonfiction novel. Instead, he decided to write a complete work of fiction based on what he'd found in the files and court-martial transcripts he had pored over for more than two years.

"I might have started writing the book with chapter two before I realized I needed a different opening," recalled Nathanson. "I'd have to go through papers and reconstruct things. But that type of writing, yes, I probably found it easier to have an example in front of me. I got documents that Dr. Milton Asbell from New Jersey had loaned me. He had been on the staff at the prison in England where executions were carried out. He had reports that he let me read, and I followed the pattern and the style of those reports. So that part in a way was easy. I had to make up all the information going in, and make up new characters because I didn't want to use the actual characters that he had written about. But that part of writing the novel was probably easier than the rest of it."

He would also include details of some of the notorious crime stories he had covered as a freelance journalist. One example concerned the memorable character of Archer Maggott. "Maggott is based on an actual person," recalled Nathanson. In a town outside of Fort Benning, Georgia, there existed Phenix City: "The story of Phenix City as a sin city goes way back, before WWII. There was a big blow-up there. The attorney general, Albert Patterson, was murdered there before he could take office. Other people were killed. Killings, all sorts of things. Anyhow, I based my character of Maggott on a couple of the people that were involved in criminal life there. It was pretty intense." It was so intense that a film entitled *The Phenix City Story* (1955) retold the events Nathanson spoke of with actor John Larch as Clem Wilson, the character Maggott was based on.

Other characters, as well as the plot, also had a basis in reality, while still others were purely the product of the author's imagination. The reason, as Nathanson explained years later, was that "To this day, I don't know if the whole thing was a latrine rumor, a true story, a cover for something else, or a figment of Russ Meyer's imagination, which I don't think. Because he worked with me early on in sending letters to former colleagues, superior officers, people he thought would be of help in locating the real people, which is what I wanted to do."

As to the work involved in creating the book, Michael Nathanson stated, "I remember asking him once when he was writing *The Dirty Dozen* if writing was hard to do. He told me it was one of the most difficult and solitary jobs he could imagine. He would tell me, 'Nothing gets done unless you do it. No one is going to write the book for you.' He was fond of a quote attributed to the Greek philosopher Epictetus: 'First, say to yourself what you would be; and then do what you have to do.'

"My father was a bit of a recluse when he was writing, spending entire days locked in his study before he would emerge sometime in the evening to prepare a cocktail and engage in some recreational reading, which he also loved to do. For many years he completely shunned television. It seemed on some days that he would never come out of his study."

A year into his project, Nathanson submitted an eight-page outline to the west coast editor of Random House and Dell Publishing without an agent but under the auspices of a friend who was trying to set up a literary packaging company. Although he was two-thirds finished with the manuscript, Nathanson recalled, "I desperately needed more money to feed my family and me and [our] cat at that time." His friend Charles Bloch had arranged the rather complicated deal between the publishing companies. Nathanson recalled, "Anyhow, about eleven months later we finally had a contract with Dell, the first contract, with the proviso that when it came to a certain point in the writing, it would be submitted to Random House for a hardcover deal, which did happen. [But it] wasn't that simple. Actually, there was contractual trouble between Dell and Random House and me and Bloch. Eventually, it was sorted out."

The idea of a film deal was considered early on as a partial manuscript was separately submitted to both Frank Sinatra and

Tony Curtis. In the interim, Nathanson kept working on characters and plot without any idea what the mission the dozen were training for would be or how to end the book.

Despite the fact that Russ Meyer had told Nathanson he saw and photographed the actual dozen, military experts had issues with the very concept. Captain Dale Dye is on record as stating, "Despite what some authors or others might tell you, it just never happened. The last thing you want in combat is some criminal bastard that you can't trust to be at your back. That's not what you need. Nobody with half an ounce of sense would do that. Nobody is going to go down to the jail and pull out people who are convicted of capital crimes like murder, rape, grand theft, and so on and so forth and put them in a unit in combat where the most important thing in the world is unity and cohesion and trust. Just not gonna happen.

"There were occasions, and have been occasions, where you'll go down to the brig or stockade and you're making a major push or effort and you've got guys who are in there for being AWOL or back talking an officer and they're doing short sentences. Then, yeah, you'll grant these guys amnesty and get them back in the ranks, because, essentially, they're good guys who just screwed the pooch and got sent to the crossbar hotel. These things happen. Do they happen to go get capital case murderers, rapists, and the like? No, under no circumstances!"

Dye also pointed out that such a possibility did exist during WWII, except it was not with the Allies. "Late in the war there was an SS Obersturmführer [Nazi first lieutenant] by the name of Oskar Dirlewanger, I think," recalled Dye. "He himself was a convicted child rapist. Wonderful guy to have as an officer, but there ya go. They were having a great problem with Yugoslavian partisans. Partisans in occupied Yugoslavia were giving the Nazis hell. They bring this SS clown in, and he goes and literally clears the prisons. He went and found pure, Aryan child molesters, formed them into a unit, and cut 'em loose on Tito's partisans in Yugoslavia. The brutality and the horror of what those people did lives long after them in the memories of the Slavs and the people that live in that region. It was never a good move, but then again, what Nazi ever made a good move? That's the story of the only real Dirty Dozen, if you will."

During the Iraq War in 1991, it was actually attempted again. Nearly two hundred prisoners serving life sentences in two different American prisons signed a petition asking to be allowed to fight, Dirty Dozen–style, against Iraq in return for a pardon. Not being a desperate Nazi army, the US Army denied the request.

The desperation that comes when one is confronted by limited resources late in a war is still prevalent. The recent events in Russia's invasion of Ukraine have resulted in similar circumstances. In September 2022, NBC reported that a Russian oligarch named Yevgeny Prigozhin was seen in a video at a prison five hundred miles east of Moscow attempting to recruit prisoners to be commandos against the Ukrainians. Much like John Reisman, he is seen telling them, "I'm taking you out of here alive but will not necessarily return you alive."

Unlike John Reisman, Prigozhin has a much more dubious past. Like Dirlewanger, Prigozhin spent nine years in prison himself in his twenties for robbery. He eventually founded and financed a company that catered events at the Kremlin, earning him the nickname "Putin's Chef." The billionaire oligarch is the reputed financier of the Wagner Group of mercenaries and has been banned from entering the US for his attempt to influence the 2018 election.

It has also been reported that Prigozhin had been recruiting prisoners for the fight in Ukraine since June 2022, calling them stormtroopers. His address to the convicts included warnings to the prisoners about the dangers of indulging in alcohol and drugs on the front lines, and also "sexual contact with local women, men, flora, fauna, anyone." The Wagner Group would be careful, he continued, about recruiting sexual offenders, before adding: "But we understand that there can be mistakes." Such bizarre statements in the face of a losing war certainly sound infinitely more like the desperate Nazis at the end of WWII than the fictionalized Dirty Dozen, but the similarities are chilling.

The Dirty Dozen was due to be published in 1965, but Nathanson continued to struggle to come up with a workable ending. Luckily, the film rights were optioned by MGM studio boss Robert O'Brien for the impressive sum of $80,000 in May, 1963. His financial woes dealt with, Nathanson was able to focus intently on a suitable resolution to his novel. Several options were considered, including having the main character, Captain John Reisman, watch from an airplane as his unit parachuted behind enemy lines into the dark night without knowing what becomes of them. Luckily, something much better occurred to Nathanson—and Hollywood would break the rules to take it even further.

2

"THE DIRTY DOZEN AWAITS"

MGM's purchase of Nathanson's unfinished manuscript was announced in the *Los Angeles Times* in a small blurb dated May 1963. Studio chief Robert Weitman was stated as the individual who acquired the rights, but it was done in conjunction with the studio's CEO, Robert O'Brien. O'Brien had been put in charge of MGM the year before, following the financial debacle of the remake of *Mutiny on the Bounty* (1962). O'Brien's résumé included being a former commissioner on the Securities and Exchange Commission; apparently, MGM's board of directors figured a straight arrow was what the studio needed to create a clean slate of original moneymakers. One of O'Brien's first would be optioning Nathanson's *The Dirty Dozen*.

Nathanson's completed manuscript ran to more than five hundred pages and was bookended by two officially written yet completely fictitious military reports. In between were characters and plot points unlike any seen in war novels at the time. His characters, both in the service of various ranks and several civilians, would be radically altered on the screen. The alterations did not please the author, but he understood why many—but certainly not all—of the changes were made. Nathanson wrote thirty-six chapters in four parts titled "The Gallows," "Les Enfants Perdus," "The Dirty Dozen," and "Kriegspiel." With that, the novel begins.

An official military report dated February 1944 details the hanging of a serviceman named Gardiner, lists those present—including one Capt. John Reisman—and explains Gardiner's crime of killing his girlfriend and her lover.

Later, Reisman is in a pub called the Butcher's Arms wondering about the other people he has killed in the world. He's described as "dark as a Spaniard or Italian, without being swarthy. His face was young yet already set and mature in the lines and hollows, and with tiny wrinkles at the eyes and mouth and forehead that belied his years. His eyes were a cold gray. Then at the bar, they had been soft brown. Maybe they could change like a chameleon or maybe they changed by themselves to cover his mood . . . [He was] not really tall for a man and had dark hair with waves in it." The thirty-year-old Reisman flirts with eighteen-year-old barmaid Tess Simmons as he wonders to himself why Gardiner was hung and not shot, as was normal military protocol.

In an earlier flashback, Franko wakes to hear the guards come for Gardiner. He then recalls his own childhood in Hell's Kitchen, the ten years he later spent in Leavenworth, and the offer he receives to join the army by boarding a ship to England. What he did to land in Marston-Tyne Prison is not yet stated.

Reisman is summoned to the OSS offices in London to meet the mustachioed fortyish Major Max Armbruster, a former college teacher. He pores over a mission he suspects did not come from Supreme Headquarters Allied Expeditionary Force (SHAEF): "Select 12 general prisoners convicted by courts-martial and doomed to be executed or serve lengthy prison terms for murder, rape, robbery, or other crimes of violence; train and qualify in as much of the clear and dirty business of behind-the-lines operations as they can in a brief but unspecified time; deliver them secretly onto the European mainland just prior to the Invasion, to wreak havoc upon segments and personnel of the Nazi war machine. This is Project Amnesty."

Reisman asks Armbruster why convicts, and is told it's hard to get men to volunteer for such a mission. Reisman is also told that, although he overstepped his orders on his previous mission, Armbruster recommended him for Project Amnesty. At the formal briefing, Reisman is joined by Armbruster, General Sam Worden, General Frances Denton of the OSS, and a surprisingly young Lieutenant Stuart Kinder. Worden takes over the meeting, mentioning the convicts. Kinder explains that the mission will also have important psychological warfare repercussions, to see the propaganda effect on the enemy and to study the effects on the men chosen for the mission. Reisman doesn't know who concocted the plan, but thinks Kinder has something to do with it.

Later that night, Reisman reads the letter he had received from his father, Aaron, an elderly Jew who married Reisman's late Catholic mother, Mary Donato. He smiles when he reads that his father wants him to settle down and not keep running around like Errol Flynn. His father mentions more about John's childhood and "the accident" that caused John to leave Chicago for good, but Reisman knows it was no accident.

Reisman goes to the Marston-Tyne Prison to meet his chosen convicts, new arrivals who've been transferred in for just this purpose. Samson Posey, a giant Native American of the Ute tribe, tried to run away before being transferred to Marston-Tyne in hopes of being shot instead of hung, so as to die honorably, like a soldier. He was caught by several guards, chained, and brought into the prison. Much background is then given about Posey's childhood, his tribe, his friends, and his prowess as a gambler. It was that prowess that sent him to prison: he killed a man he caught cheating.

MP Clyde Bowren takes Posey to the dispensary while some of the other prisoners are introduced: twenty-year-old Luis Jimenez; husky Ken Sawyer, who misses being a soldier; the slightly older Roscoe Lever, who constantly wets his lips; Archer Maggott, a tall, blond-haired, watery-eyed redneck; Myron Odell, a thin, blond, nervous-looking twenty-year-old with steel-rimmed glasses; the aforementioned Posey; Calvin Ezra Smith, a tall, thin, blue-eyed religious fanatic; and Napoleon White, the angry African American who immediately gets into a fight with Maggott that the guards break up.

Reisman meets with the lieutenant colonel who is the warden of the prison to get a little more information about the men he's chosen for the mission and about the dozen MP guards, including Corporal Bowren and the prison's hangman, Sergeant Carl Morgan. Reisman prepares to meet the group of prisoners he thinks of in terms of the French phrase "Les Enfants Perdus," which translates to "Lost Children."

Reisman then orders the prisoners to line up by size for drills. When number seven, Victor Franko, refuses, Reisman pulls him aside and whispers, "Look, you wop bastard. You don't march, I'm gonna beat the shit out of you." His back turned, Reisman waits for Franko to attack, and quickly disposes of him. Maggott tries it also, but Reisman challenges any men who won't drill to step forward. Odell considers it but then steps back. They drill for thirty minutes and are then ordered to return to their cells. Reisman prepares to meet each of them individually in hopes of figuring out by their face what each prisoner has been convicted of without checking their accompanying files.

First, he meets Napoleon White, the only African American in the dozen, who is college-educated and a former officer. White doesn't want to go on the mission, and when Reisman leaves, hoping he'll change his mind, White thinks back to his life before. In college he was a football star and had a white girlfriend, and he enlisted and attended officer candidate school after Pearl Harbor.

As for the others, Jimenez, a California fruit picker, killed a lieutenant for giving him extra guard duty. Ken Sawyer took the blame for the murder of a cabbie his friend killed while on leave. Maggott was a Phenix City hit man who raped a woman while in the service. Roscoe Lever committed a series of thefts in England, culminating in a jewelry store robbery during which he beat an old man and was caught attempting to rape the man's daughter—which, per military law, earned him a sentence of thirty years, but Reisman believes he should have gotten more.

Myron Odell was found in the presence of a dead, mutilated, half-witted woman, the murder of whom he claims to be innocent of. Glenn Gilpin's sentence is similar to Lever's, Calvin Ezra Smith clutches his Bible throughout his meeting with Reisman, Vernon Pinkley asks for time off, and Chicago native Joe Wladislaw asks if Reisman knows some of his friends. All in all, Reisman makes his choices based more on instinct than anything else.

Back in his cell, Napoleon White relives the events that led to his death sentence. As a lieutenant in charge of successfully training a Black unit in Arizona, he is transferred to Louisiana to do more of the same. On a night off, he wanders into the white section of town, where he is accosted by a drunk woman and two soldiers, one of whom has a harelip. The soldiers are made to apologize by some MPs, but when they see White walking home later that night, they drag him into their car and beat him unconscious.

The next morning, White is found by several Black soldiers in a sewer ditch, beaten, naked, and covered in feces, his scrotum slashed. He later tells the MPs who investigate that he was hit by a car and that's all he remembers. As he heals, all he cares about is finding the corporal with the harelip who beat him the most. Reassigned to train soldiers in England, White discovers the man playing poker aboard the *Ille de France*. In front of everyone on the ship, White pummels the man and slashes his throat.

It's at this moment in White's reverie that Reisman returns to ask why he didn't put up more of a defense at trial. He gives his intense hatred for white people as the reason. Reisman and White banter more until White finally agrees to join the mission.

Later that night, Reisman goes back to the pub, where he and Tess make love. In the afterglow, she asks him how he acquired the scars all over his body, allowing Reisman to detail his many mercenary and military battles. She tells him how her parents were killed in the bombing of London. Together they both agree that there is no god.

The next day, the dozen prisoners receive duffel bags containing class A uniforms and are ordered to shave and shower. Maggott refuses to shower with White, causing a fight to break out. A razor blade goes missing, prompting Bowren to conduct a strip search; the blade ultimately falls out of Lever's palm. Maggott reaches for it, but White stops him so the guards can find it.

Later, Morgan tells Reisman about the blade incident in the presence of the newly promoted Kinder. Reisman again asks Kinder who thought up the mission, and Kinder replies that he's still not sure but thinks it may have come from the British Special Training Unit (STU), in which undisciplined soldiers are pulled from the ranks to get individual specialized training, leading Kinder to believe the OSS wanted to go one better. Reisman tells Kinder he's going to look for a training spot near Colonel Everett Breed's jump school to refresh the dozen's basic training—and warns Kinder not to trust Morgan while he's gone.

Before he leaves, Reisman gathers the dozen in the basement and instructs them on maintaining total secrecy and not ever trying to escape. Afterward, Kinder comes in and passes out booklets and pencils, instructing the prisoners to write what they see on the inkblots he shows them. The images remind Posey of his tribe's mountain bear dance, at which he met his future wife, Eva Pavisook. Kinder rouses Posey from his reminiscence by asking why he hasn't written anything. Posey admits he can't write.

Reisman arrives near a beach cliff in Devonshire to scout the area when he sees a large house with a locked gate. He shoots the lock off and surveys the immense grounds of what turns out to be Stokes Manor, and Reisman likes what he sees. When he rings, the front door is answered by a testy woman named Lady Margot Strathallan and her snarling Doberman, both of whom Reisman saw earlier on the beach. He informs Lady Margot that her father has given permission for the estate's use, and after an angry back-and-forth, she relents.

On Sunday, March 5, a convoy takes Reisman, the guards,

and the prisoners to Stokes Manor. Each prisoner drives a truck, with a guard riding along as a passenger. White drives the jeep in the rear of the convoy with Reisman, who chose him because he thought it would make him feel special, but it has the opposite effect. White thinks he was chosen so he wouldn't contaminate the white trash.

They arrive at Stokes Manor in a light rain only for Reisman to see the lock on the gate has been replaced. He again pulls out his .45 and shoots. The Doberman charges Reisman, who is about to fire at him until Posey blocks his arm and then cradles the dog. Ignoring the incident, Reisman barks orders to Bowren and tells Morgan to get into fatigues because he's going to work too. When Morgan says he hasn't brought any, Reisman tells him he's going to get awfully dirty.

Work details are assigned to the men as they assemble their barracks in the rain. After lunch, Franko freaks out when he opens a crate to discover that it holds the hangman's scaffold and instructions for its erection, which he shows to his fellow prisoners. White tackles him and then asks Reisman to explain; Reisman tells them that the scaffold is simply being used for its lumber. To prove it, he takes the instructions and burns them. He then puts Franko on latrine duty. The men are also told the barracks are for the guards, and they—and Reisman—will be sleeping two to a pup tent. Bowren volunteers to play "Taps." The men converse angrily in their tents.

The following morning, Bowren instructs the men to shave in their helmets, but Maggott says he needs hot water to remove his stench. Morgan threatens him, but Maggott doesn't back down. When Bowren orders him to shave, Franko shouts that he won't shave either. Reisman steps in to tell the prisoners that they will no longer be issued shaving equipment, or hot meals . . . troublemakers will be sent back to prison. The last part frightens Franko, whose greatest fear is being sent back for his execution.

The next day, Reisman tells the dozen that they get to be soldiers again. Franko then points to Morgan and asks why he's there. Reisman tells the men what, until now, only Franko knew: that Morgan is the prison's executioner. They laugh, but decide to avoid Morgan. Reisman then marches the men out with full packs over several miles of rough terrain to the beach. They stop periodically to take notes as Reisman lectures them. When they reach the beach, Posey attempts to wash in the sea, which Franko says he shouldn't do. Instead, he tries to drink the salt water but spits it out in disgust.

After returning from their five-hour, twelve-mile trek, Reisman and Posey climb up the cliff near Stokes Manor and run an anchor line for the men to practice climbing. Odell freezes up on the line, so Reisman angrily shoots the bottom of the rope near his feet, forcing Odell to clamber to the top of the cliff. When all the men have made the climb, they go off to urinate, and Odell spots Lady Margot walking her dog. Reisman tells her she's been ordered to stay in her house. When she refuses, he threatens to call the war office and have her removed. She haughtily acquiesces.

As they have most nights, the men complain to each other about Reisman and, sometimes, what they've done to wind up in prison. Maggott tells Jimenez he was a big man in the Phenix City rackets and was drafted the day he was set to go to trial for rape. Jimenez doesn't believe him. Maggott rolls over, unable to sleep, and remembers that the crime bosses gave him up to be drafted as authorities were putting the heat on them, saying Maggott had gone too far. When Maggott gets overseas he tries to create a prostitution ring like the one he had back home, but he's moved around too much. Once he's stationed in

London, he tries again but gets ripped off. He beats the woman in anger, she screams rape, and he gets court-martialed.

On the third day of their training the weather finally clears, prompting Reisman to think the invasion may be happening soon. On the fourth day, a chipper Bowren enters Reisman's small office to announce, "The Dirty Dozen awaits!" He's joking, but Reisman tells him to have all guards address them as such.

The day begins with Reisman demonstrating hand-to-hand combat techniques, explaining their origins in the practices of Chinese monks, then using his hand to chop a piece of wood. He goes on to explain how to kill with bare hands, demonstrating on Sgt. Morgan. Reisman then teaches them how to disarm an opponent with a knife, asking Posey to be his example. Posey declines, but Reisman goads him by insulting the Ute tribe. Infuriated, Posey lunges, but Reisman drops him. Maggott, who has considerable experience with knives, steps up next, but Reisman still bests him.

Reisman explains the five basic principles and three defensive tricks for bare-handed combat and then has the men pair off to practice on each other, but not to the point of injury. They do as they're told until Maggott flips Odell harder than he should. Reisman tells Odell to make his fear work for him, and White shows Odell how to get back at Maggott. Maggott approaches again and taunts Odell, who thinks back to the girl he was accused of killing and then blacks out. Reisman forces Odell awake and asks what he did to Maggott, who's slumped on the ground nearly strangled to death. Odell shouts that he's innocent.

On Friday, March 10, Kinder arrives with his psychological test results, hoping it's not too late to change some of the men. Reisman angrily responds that they've come too far to be replaced. Kinder then explains that since the secure compound is cut off from communication, he had the Signal Corps set up a phone line. He later eats with the men and prepares to bed down in the rain in a pup tent with Reisman and the other men. Reisman explains that they're all going on a night recon using a map he made on which they must find the mistakes and mark them appropriately. Gilpin is put in charge.

During the maneuver, Franko thinks of escaping, possibly by hiding out in the manor, planning to claim that he got lost if he's caught. Running in the rainy dark, he gets belted by Bowren. When Bowren tells him he'll be hanged by Morgan, Franko begs for his life. After much thought Bowren lets Franko rejoin the others, telling him, "One chance is all you get from me." Bowren also realizes he would never want Reisman's job. The men return as scheduled, with Gilpin impressively pointing out all the map's mistakes.

Later, Reisman and Kinder talk about the psychology of the men, from Franko's killing of a man who caught him poaching to Maggott's belief that he was "mousetrapped" and Odell's constant claims of innocence. Reisman adds that the men are improving but he still has doubts. Kinder suggests testing their trustworthiness. Reisman goes to sleep while Kinder showers and then fiddles with a submachine gun to try to understand it better.

The next day, Reisman arranges for each man to meet with Kinder. White balks at the images Kinder shows him, stating there should be some Black people in them. Odell sees images of people in love and then a man with a nude woman, which causes him to freak out and say the woman was murdered. Maggott and Jimenez are also interviewed.

Following the meetings, Reisman wonders if Kinder is doing any good, especially with Odell. Since they've been training for ten days straight, Reisman puts Kinder in command so he can take some time off. He calls Tess on the phone, they meet, and they make love. Reisman promises to call her once a week.

When Reisman returns, Kinder tells him he has to leave for London that afternoon. Reisman takes over the training, bringing out two M-1 rifles. Pinkley is confused by them, but Sawyer knows them well. Reisman writes down serial numbers in order to give each man a rifle. He then instructs them to work the rifles based on the manual for thirty minutes in two groups led by White and Sawyer. An impressed Kinder is reminded by Reisman of their original order: "Their proved capability for viciousness is to be cultivated under rigid controls."

White drills the men in his group, but Maggott purposely keeps throwing off their rhythm. White lets it go for a while but finally approaches Maggott and knocks the rifle out of his hands. Reisman shows up to keep White and Maggott from killing each other. He decides to have the two teams compete, and when Maggott knocks Wladislaw's rifle from his hands, Sawyer's group wins. The men begin to respect White and hate Maggott.

In the evening, Franko grumbles to himself in the watchtower on guard duty in the rain with no ammo. When he sees Reisman, he pretends he's got him in his sights. Suddenly, he feels intense pain and blacks out. In the morning the men see Franko trussed up and tied to the tower. Reisman accepts the blame when the men cut Franko down and asks him what he would have done if he'd had ammo. He doesn't respond.

Lady Margot, feeling restless, calls Reisman several times to invite the men to Sunday tea. Reisman finally answers and politely turns her down, but later rethinks the invitation and decides to accept. He asks Lady Margot if he and one of the men can come to the house to borrow games, books, etc. to entertain the men.

Reisman and White—who calls himself "Jones"—arrive and make polite conversation as Lady Margot gives them a chess set, playing cards, checkers, and five books chosen by White. As they leave, Margot requests permission to walk on the beach again, and Reisman doesn't grant it. She angrily slams the door.

As they drive back to their compound in their jeep, Reisman prods White about the books he chose: a history book by Arnold Toynbee, poetry by Rudyard Kipling, *Winnie the Pooh* by A. A. Milne, and books by T. E. Lawrence and Joseph Conrad. When they arrive, Reisman removes the jeep's rotor as usual, prompting White to say that Reisman still doesn't trust the men. Reisman replies, "Would you?"

In the barracks, Reisman and White join the men and guards in enjoying a meal Jimenez has prepared. Reisman later presses White to answer his question about trust, and White says maybe. Reisman prods him further, and White says not yet. At the same time, an irate Lady Margot walks near the compound with her Doberman and gets the dog to chew through the phone line.

Back in the barracks, Posey rushes to do the dishes so he can join the others in a poker game. Reisman gets Morgan to play checkers with Franko. The poker chips are bullets provided by Reisman that must be returned later. After the first hour, Posey is ahead, followed by Reisman and Maggott in third. Hating to lose to Posey, Maggott begins to palm the high cards and hides them behind his knee. He deals the last hand and raises the bet. When he pulls out a royal flush, Posey pretends to yawn and stretch and pulls the cards out from behind Maggott's knee. A fight ensues, with both men using the judo they'd been taught. Reisman has them fight outside to a draw, now that Posey has learned to control his temper. The stalemate ends with them shaking hands.

The next three days are filled with more drills and practice disassembling and reassembling rifles and pistols blindfolded. When Reisman moves the parts around, only White, Sawyer, and Maggott figure it out. They all do it again and succeed. Reisman collects the weapons and replaces them with M-3 grease guns.

Bowren returns from the quartermaster with supplies and a manila folder containing a message from Kinder telling Reisman the phone is dead and sergeant stripes for Bowren. They check the phone line to see that it's been chewed, and Reisman knows it was Lady Margot's doing. The line is repaired and Reisman calls Kinder, who tells him a CID man named Leon Osterman has been asking for him.

The next day, Reisman is amazed to see former Chicago detective Osterman in his office. They reminisce about Reisman's early years, including the incident that occurred when he was sixteen. Reisman decides to tell Osterman about his mission and asks for his help with Odell. The guards have taken to calling him "Pope," since he constantly says that he's innocent.

Odell is summoned and Osterman relaxes him enough so he can tell his side of the story. He became a medic in Glasgow to avoid combat duty and was what's termed a "short arm inspector"—someone who checks soldiers for STDs. Odell recounts a lengthy series of events that culminate in his finding himself blacked out in the presence of the naked dead woman. When Osterman asks if he's blacked out since, Odell mentions his recent tangle with Maggott. He discusses his childhood growing up in a Catholic orphanage, where the blackouts first occurred. They talk some more, and Odell is dismissed.

Osterman and Reisman continue to discuss Odell's case until Osterman asks Reisman if he remembers what happened in 1930. Reisman is wary of discussing the incident, but since Osterman was involved, they recall the event that forever changed the course of Reisman's life. It also resulted in Reisman's committing murder.

3

"I'M GUILTY! MY GOD, I'M GUILTY!"

In the summer of 1930, sixteen-year-old John Reisman was enjoying spending time at his favorite after-school hangout in his Chicago neighborhood. The store was run by an old man named Tanner. Tanner also ran numbers on the side, and one day three local hoods came in to persuade him to stop. Young Reisman was present when the old man was beaten, and when he tried to stop the thugs, he too was beaten and then thrown out of the store.

Reisman suffered his guilt in silence until Tanner died in the hospital from his wounds. No longer able to contain his secret, Reisman told Leon Osterman, at that time a police officer. Osterman assured Reisman that he had done the right thing, but Reisman remained gripped by fear and guilt.

One fateful night Reisman was cornered by the thug who had beaten him the most. The teenager was dragged into an alley below the El train and beaten again. They struggled until a gun fell from his assailant's coat pocket. Reisman snatched it up and emptied the gun into the thug's body as the sound of a passing train muffled the gunshots.

When reminded of the incident, Osterman again reassures Reisman that he did the right thing, which is why he protected him and got him a job on the docks. He also reminds Reisman that he was able to catch the other two culprits after Reisman went to sea. Reisman's guilt over killing in self-defense is hardly relieved, however.

The night before informing the men they'll be receiving live ammo, Reisman sends them out on patrol in two groups led by Sawyer and Franko. The men are sent without guards, and Reisman and Kinder wonder if that was the right thing to do.

While on patrol, Franko leads his men to where the firing range has been set up for the next day's use. He begins to think of a way to use the live ammo to their advantage for escape. Posey sees where Franko is and reports back to Sawyer, and they agree to listen in on what Franko says. Franko explains that when the time is right, they should kill the officers and guards, bury them, and then go to the manor to do the same to Lady Margot. Franko's patrol, which includes White, reluctantly agrees. Sawyer, after hearing everything, pulls back and asks his men if they should go along. Not entirely sure, they decide to sleep on it.

On the way to target practice the next morning, the men are eerily silent. Kinder is extremely apprehensive, and Reisman sees cigarette butts on the ground near the targets. Following a gun inspection, Reisman gives instructions for the firing range. The guards fire first as an example while Odell, Franko, White, and Sawyer wait for their ammo. Reisman purposely puts himself in the line of fire between the prisoners and their targets. Kinder and Morgan are in an observational position as Bowren gives the signal to fire, which no one does. Several tense moments pass until Franko fires at the actual target. He smiles to himself, knowing he can pick his moment when ready.

Reisman requests that Kinder set things up for them all to go to Colonel Breed's jump school. Kinder then asks how the bad blood between Reisman and Breed began. In Italy, when Breed was still a major, Reisman, dressed in civilian clothes, infiltrated Breed's outfit as they bivouacked in a small village following a battle. When Reisman gave Breed a hard time about not letting his men have some fun, Breed angrily asked for Reisman's ID and put him under arrest. When Reisman's ID checked out, Breed was forced to release Reisman, which he did begrudgingly. After hearing the tale, Kinder suggests that Reisman play to Breed's ego, and then leaves for London. Reisman goes to see Tess and they again make love. Reisman asks her what she thinks of the idea of getting a woman for his men, and she likes it.

Reisman instructs Bowren to go into town and find a prostitute for the dozen. He then remembers Breed's reaction when he suggested the same to him: Breed stated angrily that women had no place in a military man's life, which was why he was divorced. When Bowren returns with a drunken prostitute for the men, Reisman has Bowren set her up in the small office used for paperwork and the like.

Reisman tells the men that they each have fifteen minutes, no more. Odell is first in but then runs out immediately. Next is Franko, who overstays his fifteen minutes. Jimenez follows and boasts of doing it twice. Smith feels guilty, while Posey and White refuse. When Maggott thinks the woman has been with White, he beats and rapes her until Bowren drags him off. Bowren then drives the woman away while Reisman burns the bedsheets and buries the ashes.

When the men's convoy arrives at Breed's jump school,

Franko's good mood fades when he sees the jump tower and watches a man drop. Breed then asks Reisman if the general Kinder said would be joining them would like to review his troops. Reisman goes to the back of a truck and grabs Sawyer, who, once instructed, quickly and silently reviews Breed's men. He then retreats with his cohorts, who laugh uproariously.

Called into Breed's office, Reisman is given a severe dressing down, but he refuses to tell Breed who the men are and what their mission is. He simply requests the use of two of Breed's men to help train the dozen in an expedited two-week jump course. As Reisman leaves, Breed mentions that he's friends with Lady Margot, who told him she heard a woman scream the previous night. Reisman merely says it was one of his men being tortured.

The dozen's jump training then begins in earnest. After long runs and exercises over the next few days, the men are exhausted. On the second day, strapped into harnesses, they practice jumping from an elevated platform that simulates an airplane door. When Wladislaw is attacked by two of Breed's men in the latrine, he takes them both on. He wins the battle but is badly beaten. Reisman denies being involved and asks Wladislaw about the attack, but Wladislaw still thinks Reisman is responsible.

On the fourth day, Reisman realizes it's Good Friday and tells the men they can attend church services. All agree to go except Posey. When Reisman adds that they will have to shave and shower, no one goes.

Their training accelerates, and Reisman and his men now jump with parachutes from the high jump tower. Franko is assigned to attach Reisman's parachute and release it on command from the ground. Breed takes over from Franko and purposely leaves Reisman hanging in midair. After a lengthy wait,

Reisman finally gets the command and lands safely. When he does, he turns off Breed's microphone and proceeds to curse him out. Breed threatens to court-martial him for insubordination, and Reisman tells him to turn on the mic and he'll say it all again. Breed walks away in disgust.

When it's Franko's turn to jump, he's naturally scared at first. However, he thinks that if he injures himself in the jump, he won't have to go on the mission. He purposely comes down too fast and inadvertently lands on Morgan. Reisman angrily berates Franko and tells him to apologize. Franko refuses.

On Easter Sunday, Bowren is eager to go to church. Reisman allows the guards to go as well, but when he sees Reisman alone with the men, Bowren changes his mind and stays. The dozen take advantage of their day off and lounge around. For the first time, Reisman doesn't carry his rifle when he's with the men, and even persuades Franko and Morgan to play checkers together.

Leon Osterman shows up in uniform later that day to tell Reisman that Odell's victim may have committed suicide, as she had attempted it before. Osterman is investigating unofficially and tells Reisman that it's going to take a while. He suggests taking Odell back to the crime scene. Reisman says he may do so after next week, because Odell is getting stronger.

On jump day, Morgan chickens out, and Reisman says he'll take his stripes. Breed sidles up to Morgan on the ground and questions him, and Morgan absentmindedly gives up his name and rank.

Over the next three days, the men jump once a day and continue their strenuous exercise program. Kinder is summoned from London to watch the fourth jump and is impressed. Breed shows up after they've all landed, mocks Reisman again, and leaves. The dozen and Kinder agree to hate him.

On the morning of Saturday, April 15, Kinder leaves and Reisman sends Bowren to buy wings for the men, and to procure another prostitute. He then calls Armbruster to say they're ready for anything.

At the Baker Street offices of the OSS, Denton conducts a briefing with Reisman, Armbruster, and Kinder. Denton says the day and place of the invasion are not yet known, which prompts Reisman to ask if his men are central to its success. This angers Denton, and he calls them the icing on the cake. Denton then describes one possible mission in which the dozen would go undercover as Nazis. When Reisman says he has a Black soldier and a Ute, Denton tells him to replace them, then finishes the briefing and leaves.

Reisman implores Armbruster to get him another mission for his men, and the Major mentions a château in France where Nazi officers meet to plan *Kriegsspiels*—war games—and relax. Reisman wants it, but Armbruster says it's just a rumor, and if it were true, a first-rate team would do it, not the dozen. In addition, SHAEF doesn't know when or if *Kriegsspiels* are planned, but Armbruster promises to find out more about it.

Meanwhile, Breed has had Morgan traced and now knows about the dozen. He drives to Stokes Manor with a truck full of men. Breed confronts Bowren at the front gate and tells him to bring Morgan out. Bowren returns with Morgan, and when Breed threatens to bust him, Morgan opens the gate. White thinks it's a Reisman trick, but Wladislaw sees the men who jumped him at Breed's camp. White doesn't care and passes the word that they should all be quiet. When asked for their name, rank, serial number, and organization, they give only their unit number. Breed takes Morgan aside and threatens him; Morgan tells him what he knows, which is next to nothing.

Reisman sneaks into camp with explosives while Breed has

the wings torn off the dozen. Breed tells Franko to shave, but he refuses. White starts toward the men holding Franko when Reisman sets off three explosions. He gives away his position on the roof when he yells to Breed to have his men give up their weapons or be shot for trespassing in a maximum-security area. The troops surrender their weapons to Bowren and White while Breed and Reisman go into Reisman's office to talk. They verbally spar until Reisman declares a stalemate and challenges Breed to a war game maneuver. Breed agrees.

After Breed leaves, Bowren tells Reisman that Morgan let Breed in and the two acted like old friends. Reisman calls the men and guards to fall in and personally apologizes to each one. He calls Morgan over and strips him of his weapons angrily, telling him he's going back to Marston-Tyne to be tried and convicted. As he leaves, Morgan mutters, "You'll get yours, Captain." Franko mutters the same to Morgan.

Bowren and the other guards drive Morgan to prison; only Bowren returns, as the fewer people who know of the work from now on, the better. The dozen now move into the guards' empty barracks. They pick cots and then go to the mess tent, where Reisman tells them about the impending war games. They're all for it as revenge. White asks about the invasion, and Reisman says war games first or they won't be part of the invasion. They agree not to follow rules and that Reisman won't be involved. Reisman tries to talk them into shaving and cleaning up. Posey agrees first, followed by Sawyer and White and then Franko, who had started the no-shaving routine in the first place.

At the end of April Reisman receives two letters. The first is from Osterman, who apologizes for being in Scotland and says he'll work on Odell's case in mid-May. The second is from the commandant of the prison, who explains to Reisman why Morgan won't be tried and will retain his rank.

Reisman drives to London three days before the war games to meet Armbruster, Kinder, Denton, and a nervous civilian. Denton introduces the civilian as Monsieur Lemaire, former caretaker of the Château de la Villain in Rennes. He's told Denton that most Nazi generals can be found at the château for one or two nights at the start of each month. Lemaire says the château is normally guarded by troops from occupied countries, but when the officers are there it's secured by crack German troops. Reisman loves it, but Denton explains it's still a suicide mission.

At war games HQ, Reisman listens to the chatter and explosions as Bowren tells him a barrage is scheduled for 08:55 twenty yards from Breed's command post. Reisman says the men will have time to meet up. Kinder shows up at headquarters to tell Reisman what a great job he did cleaning up the dozen, as he almost didn't recognize them. Reisman hopes Breed has the same problem.

White is in command in the field with Franko, Jimenez, Pinkley, and Armbruster as an observer. Armbruster is surprised by how well he's gotten along with the dozen—all on the same team now—after having fitted them all with the equipment they needed, including timed pencil explosives. It's 08:54. Four men come down during the explosions, with Odell landing near White, cursing.

White checks a clearing and believes he sees Breed's command post. The dozen switch from red armbands to blue. Sawyer uses forged papers and green observer armbands to steal a jeep and a machine gun, picking Maggott and Gilpin up along the way. Armbruster chooses to stay with White as the dozen split up. Sawyer and some others take the jeep into a ditch and fake a crash, burning some of Posey's uniform and putting bandages on him.

Breed and some troops meet them on the road, and Sawyer says they need an ambulance. Posey is brought to Breed's bunker and Odell cares for him, taking his boots off, slipping in timed pencil explosives, and placing the boots under the radio table. Sawyer and Gilpin remove packs with more timed pencil explosives in them and are seen by the visiting Denton. Meanwhile, White hijacks the ambulance and drives it to the command post to capture Breed, saying, "Captain Reisman's compliments." The plan B pencil explosives are deactivated.

At HQ, Reisman, Bowren, and Kinder hear the radio announcer say, "They did it!" The announcer then says, "Disregard previous message," followed by an hour's silence. They drive to Breed's post, where Breed tells them Reisman should honor his agreement as the umpire claims that the dozen flagrantly disregarded the rules. Reisman asks where his men are, and Breed tells him they're under armed guard in a truck. Breed wants Reisman to vacate Stokes Manor immediately. Reisman asks for two weeks, then goes to find the men still under guard and chatting with Bowren. Reisman goes to Denton, who tells him the umpire doesn't matter and the Rennes mission is his. Denton says the dozen should relish it, explaining that a normal unit wouldn't be as bloodthirsty. Reisman responds that his men may be a little more lost but are just like any soldiers.

Back at the compound, Reisman pours scotch all around. When Reisman asks if they'd like to get a bagful of generals, Franko asks, "Ours or theirs?" Reisman answers, "Does it make any difference?" He then explains the mission bluntly, using a model château sent by Kinder. Franko likes the plan, thinking he can escape or be captured and sit out the war no matter who wins. Reisman offers them all a chance to back out and tells them to sleep on it, because once they're committed, that's it.

Not satisfied by simply training the men with the model,

Reisman decides to have them dress in Nazi uniforms and return the books they borrowed from Stokes Manor without being caught or encountering Lady Margot. He asks White to return with volume 2 of Toynbee's *A Study of History* as proof they were there. The men return in an hour, and White explains that Lever picked the lock. Reisman says they'll do it again the next night, with each man bringing back something from a different room.

Lady Margot hears them on both nights and, in fear, sets her dog loose. Posey gets into the bedroom, steals a photo, and runs out to the others. Gilpin and Odell lock the dog out to sneak back in and steal some more. Posey shows the photo to Reisman, who sees it's of a German officer.

Breed and Lady Margot show up the next morning demanding that Reisman leave. Instead, Reisman shares the items stolen from her home with Breed. Seeing the photo, Breed asks who it is. Lady Margot responds that it's her lover. Breed and Reisman walk outside, and after Reisman prods him, Breed says he won't say anything. They agree to leave Lady Margot alone, and Breed drives off.

Osterman checks in on May 20 and asks Reisman to bring Odell to Glasgow. Reisman agrees, even though it will be cutting it close to the time of the mission. They take a cab to the VD clinic where Odell worked. Odell is instructed to go inside for fifteen to twenty minutes, remember what happened, and then come out and talk about it. He goes in nervously, sees the rooms, then darts out a back door to the alley.

Odell hails a cab and asks the driver where he can get laid. The cabbie takes him to a woman's flat, which Odell enters nervously. The woman, Mrs. Nora Barnes, treats him warmly. They chat as she pours him some brandy, and Odell confesses to being a virgin. He begins to picture the girl from the clinic.

Nora leaves and returns wearing only a slip and stockings. When she undresses Odell, he feels the same old pain in his groin he's always felt when sexually aroused. She caresses him and then mounts him, and after a while, he orgasms.

On Sunday morning Odell travels forty miles south to a church. A priest hears his confession, which is more like a boast about how he's finally done it and it felt so good they did it three times. He receives a surprisingly light penance and goes to Mass. He then makes his way back amid the growing movement of troops and equipment.

Kinder puts the dozen on alert to leave on May 31 for the airfield at Breed's post. He waits while Reisman goes through the attack plan using the model, then notices there are eleven men, not twelve. The dozen know nothing about it, but Reisman tells Kinder what happened and that Osterman is discreetly searching for Odell. Kinder wants to report it, but Reisman asks him not to and Kinder agrees.

As they're dismantling the compound, Bowren sees Odell return. When Reisman asks why he came back, Odell eventually tells him with pride that he still thinks he's innocent, but it doesn't matter anymore. Reisman asks Odell if he got laid, and Odell says, "Damn right, Captain."

All the supplies are piled up for the corps of engineers except the scaffold crate. Reisman calls Franko over, lights his lighter, gives it to him, and says, "Burn it."

Reisman and the dozen set up camp on Breed's airfield. Armbruster and Denton fly in from London for a final briefing and confirm that the invasion is set for Monday, June 5, weather permitting. The dozen lounge on the tarmac, cleaning their guns and trying to hear the officers' conversation. Denton says they'll leave Sunday night, and if there's a delay, they'll receive a coded message of "Bowsprit." There's no alternate target if the generals aren't there, so if the mission is called off, they're to bury their supplies and find a way back.

Denton is unsure that Reisman can pass for a German and doesn't know whether he can trust the dozen, but Reisman reassures him. Armbruster offers Reisman cyanide pills but he refuses them, saying the dozen may kill each other but not themselves.

Reisman briefs the men on the area of the château. When they ask how to get out, especially if Reisman is dead, he tells them to improvise. He tells them to write letters home, which Reisman does as well. Everyone but Odell writes the letters, even Posey.

Posey has a dream that night about a traditional Ute sun dance that he takes as a sign. He goes to Reisman to ask for certain materials to perform the sun dance. Reisman tells him to improvise with whatever Kinder can scrounge for him. Chaplains arrive to offer help, but Reisman intercepts them so Posey can dance the sun dance uninterrupted.

Posey dances all day and night into June 3. He neither drinks nor eats. On the last morning of his dance, it rains. Dejected, he goes to his pup tent to eat and sleep, thinking he's failed because he didn't have the right materials. On June 4 the rain worsens, and Reisman gets the "Bowsprit" message. Posey offers to stop the rain using the power he got from the sun dance and tries again, praying all morning without food in the gale. Reisman gets a dispatch, reads it, and tells Posey it worked: the dispatch says the sky will be clear tonight when they go and again the next day for the invasion.

That night they prepare to board the plane. Bowren and Kinder say goodbye, but then Bowren sneaks onto the plane with his equipment. Later, when Reisman goes to check with the pilot on their ETA, he sees Bowren hiding in a storage area. Reisman tells him to parachute out, but Bowren reminds him that they're over the English Channel. Farther out over the channel, the men change into Nazi uniforms and collect their weapons.

Reisman is apprehensive but understands why. He sees fear in Bowren, but the dozen are surprisingly calm. The jumpmaster asks what they did to deserve such a dirty job, and Reisman answers, "It's not what they did to deserve the job. It's that the job to be done deserves us." Bowren jumps first and Reisman goes last, hearing the flak in the distance from a diversionary attack on a rail yard.

Once inside the château, Odell waits in the closet of a suite he was assigned to be in. He knows Reisman and Sawyer, posing as Nazi officers, have made it in using forged papers. Others of the dozen are in their prearranged rooms while some wait outside to do what they need to do when the explosives set by Sawyer and Reisman in the *Kriegsspiel* room go off. When that happens, Odell is to burst through the halls and rooms, killing anyone he encounters, and meet Reisman in the motor park. Maggott, Posey, and Jimenez volunteered to attack the roadblock. Guard post sentries are shot point-blank with silencers by Franko and Wladislaw, who then replace them.

Knowing Pinkley and Smith have killed the boathouse sentries, White stands on the balcony of a detached service building, silenced pistol in hand, watching a card game going on inside. He then sees a German general's limo enter the courtyard. He looks back at the card players and knows he's no longer as angry as he'd been in prison.

Lever is hiding in a room when a French maid comes in, making him think of the woman he attacked in the jewelry store. As the maid is about to leave, he grabs her, muzzles her, and throws her on the bed. They argue in pidgin German and

French. Lever doesn't see her reach into her bag for a pair of scissors, which she plunges into his chest.

Odell hears a couple enter the suite he's in, laughing and talking. The woman comes into the bedroom and, when she opens the closet, Odell stabs her, finally remembering what happened with the naked girl in Glasgow. He shouts, "I'm guilty! My God, I'm guilty!" He runs out of the closet and the officer shoots him in the shoulder. Odell shoots back with his Schmeisser in one hand and a knife in the other, then runs down the hallway shouting that he's guilty.

Nathanson now ends the story the way he began it: with an official report detailing the events of the attack on the château. Dated June 15, 1944, and written by Major Stuart Kinder, it's labeled a top-secret OSS report to Colonel Francis Denton and Major Max Armbruster.

The primary source for the information in the report is Sergeant Clyde Bowren, hospitalized in Normandy on June 14. Bowren, gravely wounded and unconscious, is listed as AWOL but Kinder says he should be promoted to staff sergeant and transferred to OSS with recommendations. The French Underground also provided information for the report, and some events have been inferred based on the passage of time.

Odell, Lever, Smith, Gilpin, and Franko are confirmed dead, and Bowren, White, Jimenez, and Reisman are listed as wounded (with Jimenez, White, and Reisman also shown to be missing). Posey, Sawyer, Wladislaw, Pinkley, and Maggott are missing in action. Kinder then explains the mission again and opines that no other outfit would've performed as well.

The mission started early with six dead sentries. Reisman had learned that the war game was scheduled for the next morning when more generals would be there, but since some had arrived early, Reisman acted. At least two important generals were confirmed killed. At the motor park, Pinkley told Bowren he personally shot several officers trying to escape via the boat-house and the river. He shot one of them after hearing Franko following him and shouting to him in German and English. Pinkley examined the body, saw it was a general, and asked why Franko was yelling at him. When Franko explained that they could have escaped with him, Pinkley put his weapon in Franko's belly and said, "Don't try it, Vic."

As Reisman helped the wounded Bowren, he saw Gilpin destroy the radio antenna. Gilpin was then machine-gunned as he climbed down the roof after shooting from there. Smith was killed at the powerhouse after taking down six Germans.

White and the others were waiting for Reisman in the motor park, with White wounded in his side but able to walk. They wanted to split up to escape, but Reisman made them stay to attend to the wounded before taking one of the limos. Sawyer, Wladislaw, Maggott, and Jimenez set up a defense perimeter. Franko and Pinkley fell back, and Posey was back a little farther should relief troops appear. As Reisman dressed White's wounds, White said he killed all the guards in the card room for his own reasons. They had called him "*Schwartze.*"

Jimenez was ordered to cover the boathouse with Pinkley, Wladislaw, and Sawyer, but he saw Posey was outnumbered and, without orders, raced to help him. Bowren put himself, White, and Franko in the limo with Reisman driving and Maggott firing from the passenger seat. Flares illuminated Posey as Jimenez got near him but was shot in the thigh and fell. Posey, who had stripped to the waist and applied war paint, kept firing a heavy German machine gun. When Jimenez reached him, Posey threw him aside and kept firing.

Franko asked Reisman to surrender to the Germans at the

barricade. When Reisman wouldn't, Franko aimed his weapon at Reisman. Bowren shot him twice in the neck with his .45.

The information in the report then becomes sketchy, as Bowren kept slipping in and out of consciousness, but he knows they encountered some Germans. Help came from the French Underground, and Reisman ordered Maggott to care for White. They were very near where the Americans had landed when Reisman told Bowren this was the end of the tour and left.

The report concludes with recommendations that this type of operation never be attempted again, and that all personnel involved be returned to active duty at their previous rank.

Thus ended the tale of Mick Nathanson's Dirty Dozen. The book was optioned by MGM in 1963 while still incomplete and published by Random House two years later. MGM CEO Robert O'Brien put a team together so the finished film might be released in time for the book's paperback publication by Dell. The initial team wouldn't last long on the project, but the headaches and revisions involved in its production certainly would.

4

THE MOST MISERABLE SON OF A BITCH ANYONE HAS EVER SEEN

The team that MGM executive Robert O'Brien put together consisted of several movie veterans under contract at the studio. *The Dirty Dozen* was to be produced by William Perlberg and directed by George Seaton.

Seaton, best known for the Christmas classic *Miracle on 34th Street* (1947), actually got his start in show business in the early 1930s. As one of the first actors to portray the Lone Ranger on radio, legend has it he created the popular phrase "Hi-yo, Silver!" because he couldn't whistle as the script required. He also wrote several plays, and when one was read by an MGM executive, he was put under contract in 1933. Through the next several decades he worked in various genres for all the major studios, and in 1945 he teamed up with producer William Perlberg at 20th Century-Fox on his first venture as a director. It was the Betty Grable musical *Diamond Horseshoe*, which Seaton also wrote. By 1950 the two men worked together exclusively, forming their own production company.

Perlberg, a Jewish immigrant who came to the United States from Poland in 1925, got his start in show business as an agent for the William Morris Agency and later as a personal assistant to Columbia Pictures' Harry Cohn. He became a producer in 1935 and, like Seaton, had a string of box office successes over the next three decades for all the major studios. Clearly, the two veterans seemed like a good team to make *The Dirty Dozen* a box-office winner.

Seaton and Perlberg had made films that were similar but hardly identical to *The Dirty Dozen*, including the Korean War action film *The Bridges at Toko-Ri* (1954) and the WWII spy thriller *The Counterfeit Traitor* (1962), both starring William Holden and both big hits for their studios. The two men had several other projects lined up around the same time, including yet another WWII spy thriller, *36 Hours* (1964), starring James Garner, which also revolved around the D-Day invasion. The schedule for *The Dirty Dozen* seemed tight but workable as Perlberg announced in the May 14, 1964, issue of the *Hollywood Reporter* that Henry Denker was working on the script and would be finished by the end of the week.

Denker had been a successful lawyer during the Depression, establishing several successful precedents in workers' compensation cases. He had also dabbled in writing, and by 1945 wrote full-time. It didn't matter the medium, as he wrote prolifically for radio, film, novels, plays, and even early television. Some of his work was based on his law experience, while other projects had a more religious slant or, in some cases, a medical crisis.

The problem with his screenplay for *The Dirty Dozen* was first noticed by Mick Nathanson. "I met him when I wasn't even finished with the novel," recalled Nathanson. "It was so easy to move forward, and MGM had an option on the book already. It wasn't completed but they had the option. They brought in Denker and we met one day in Los Angeles. I was living there then. He questioned me and then he went off and did his thing. He had no knowledge of my novel whatsoever. He was a tough-looking bastard. It was just awful."

One of the many problems Nathanson had with Denker's script was the fact that he completely made up the climax, having the dozen raid and slaughter the inhabitants of Peenemünde rocket station in Germany, where the V-2 rocket was developed. The site was populated by German scientists and their wives and children. Nathanson had not yet written his own climax, but what he had in mind wasn't even close to being as graphic.

Because it was his baby, Nathanson took matters into his own hands: "I called Perlberg, who was then the producer. I said, 'You can't do this. It's awful. There are thousands of reasons. Why don't you let me do a screenplay?' He said, 'Come on in and talk to me.' He was a bulldog of a man. So, I came in and talked to him. I had my list of what was wrong, all these different things that are wrong. Boom, boom, boom! He asked, 'Can you write a screenplay?' 'I never have, but there's no reason why I can't.'" Not sure how much to ask for, Nathanson was advised by his then lawyer to find out and be sure not to ask for too much, or he would price himself out of the deal. If he asked for too little, he would be viewed as a novice. When he discovered the standard was only $15,000, Nathanson begrudgingly took on the task.

With very little knowledge of how to go about it, Nathanson began to write a screenplay based on his novel. The time it took him to finish the draft was somewhere between four and six months, which meant a schedule conflict might be looming with the soon-to-be filmed *36 Hours*. However, Nathanson's finished draft also proved to be problematic in that it ran to nearly two hundred pages. "In the screenplay that I wrote, I started it before the novel opens," recalled the author. "I had a half dozen scenes of the Dirty Dozen before they committed [any] crime. They're about to commit or in the middle of committing the crime. With Napoleon White/Robert Jefferson, he's aboard a ship on [its] way to Europe, and he spots the soldier, the corporal who has done him wrong. It was a racial thing. He spots him and goes after him with a knife and slits his throat right there on the ship. . . . We understand, I understood his crime. . . . Then five or six of the others I discover in the middle of their crime. This is before the credits. Then, finally, I forget what the main opening scene was, but it opens up into the story. I liked it a lot, but nothing happened [with] it."

By April of 1964, while Nathanson struggled with the script, director George Seaton was considering casting and location options. Nick Adams was under serious consideration for the role of the rebellious Chicago gangster, Victor Franko. He may also have been considered for the restructured role of Joseph Wladislaw, as he was also of Ukrainian heritage and had worked in a coal mine as a child. Seaton had worked with Adams previously but ultimately passed on the troubled young actor. A few years later, after appearing in several low-budget Japanese horror films, Adams died under mysterious circumstances at the age of thirty-six.

Also under consideration at the time by Seaton was the number-one African American film star, Sidney Poitier. No reason has been given as to why the legendary Poitier was not hired, but his career, unlike that of Nick Adams, certainly did not suffer in any way. Seaton was also preparing to film most if not all of *The Dirty Dozen* in and around Europe.

Unfortunately, by December 1964, because of the extra time it took for Nathanson to write the screenplay, Seaton announced that he was ending his contract with MGM, for-going its final three years. He would, however, still direct the other MGM film in which he had invested more time, *36 Hours*. Perlberg would join Seaton in January the following year, also leaving *The Dirty Dozen*.

The Cannes Film Festival that year was abuzz about a new non–James Bond film starring Sean Connery that was to be distributed by MGM in the United States. Directed by vet-eran New York director Sidney Lumet, *The Hill* (1965) was an unusual film with a practically all-British cast that was caus-ing quite a stir. It concerned a WWII–era squad of military prisoners trying to survive torturous conditions in the blis-tering desert, as well as the hypocritical hierarchy of British military life. It would go on to tie for the Best Screenplay at Cannes for writers R. S. Allen and Ray Rigby, whose life inspired the gritty tale.

Connery's performance as Trooper Joe Roberts, the most rebellious and courageous of the prisoners, was considered a revelation to filmgoers, despite the fact that he was not originally considered for the role. Studio executives wanted the likes of Burt Lancaster or Tony Curtis for the role. The film's American producer thought the idea was ludicrous and reminded the executives that the characters were all British, suggesting—and actually getting—Connery for the role. That producer's name was Ken Hyman.

Born Malcolm Kenneth Hyman into movie royalty, Hyman is the son of wily film executive Eliot Hyman. Eliot had formed Associated Artists Productions (aap) in 1948 and two years later became the sole owner. By 1954, having acquired the entire library of Warner Bros. films and cartoons, he syn-dicated them to television. He later cofounded Seven Arts and produced several high-profile, controversial but moneymaking films, such as Stanley Kubrick's *Lolita* (1962) and John Fran-kenheimer's *Seven Days in May* (1964).

Eliot Hyman's head of UK operations was his son Ken. Born in New York City on December 11, 1928, Ken and his two younger brothers, Frederick and Michael, grew up in Westport, Connecticut. He and his brother Fred both went into the family business, with Fred eventually moving on to co-create and run the Cousteau Society.

After a stint in the Marines, Ken followed in his father's footsteps. He worked to produce several Hammer horror films, such as *The Hound of the Baskervilles* (1959) and *The Terror of the Tongs* (1961). According to Hyman, "I was the liaison between New York and Hammer Films. I decided I'd like to try making a movie. So, I bought the film rights from the Conan Doyle estate to remake *Baskervilles*. When I went back to England, I pitched the idea, and they liked it. That was my introduction to producing."

His father's Seven Arts company gave him opportunities to grow in the business. He was credited as executive producer for the Chaplinesque Jackie Gleason vehicle *Gigot* (1962), and earned the same credit working with Robert Aldrich for the first time on *What Ever Happened to Baby Jane?* for Warner Bros. that same year. The lanky Hyman's flair for producing offbeat projects gained momentum.

The release of *The Hill* three years later continued to change the course of Hyman's career. Now long retired to the English countryside with his wife, Caroline, Hyman recalled in 2021, "Bob O'Brien had seen *The Hill* and kind of liked it. . . . In any event, he had a script and asked if I'd like to produce it. . . . I told him I had to read the material, as I wasn't familiar with it. I read the script, then scanned and read the book. . . . I had read the play *The Hill* by Ray Allen and liked it. Having been in the service myself, I knew guys like those characters, as I did with *The Dirty Dozen*."

As the newly assigned producer of the project, Hyman suggested to O'Brien that another writer should tackle the script. "I suggested Nunnally Johnson for the script, as he was a friend of mine," Hyman said. "He had a wonderful sense of humor and was a wonderful writer." O'Brien was at first reticent, believing the prolific and well-known Johnson to be more of a comedy writer. Johnson had indeed penned the likes of *How to Marry a Millionaire* (1953) and several other lighter films. Hyman was quick to remind O'Brien that Johnson was nominated for an Oscar for his screenplay for *The Grapes of Wrath* (1940) and was also the scribe for *The Man in the Gray Flannel Suit* (1956) and *The Three Faces of Eve* (1957), both of which the versatile Johnson also directed. Although an action war film, *The Dirty Dozen*'s themes of redemption and loyalty convinced O'Brien that Johnson could write the screenplay.

Despite being in his mid-sixties at the time, Johnson was up to the challenge, as long as he was able to write the screenplay in his own fashion. "Kenny Hyman called me when I was in New York," Johnson recalled in 1969. "He sent me a book called *The Dirty Dozen* and wanted me to do the script. I read it and thought it was good, exciting stuff."

Several obstacles existed for Johnson, though. He would not be back in London for another month, and Hyman wanted to work closely with him on the project. The stipulation that he work as he wished was nonnegotiable to the veteran writer of more than fifty films, mostly at 20th Century-Fox under the auspices of Darryl F. Zanuck. As Johnson later explained: "I said, 'Look, Kenny, you're a good friend of mine. As far I'm concerned, you've given me a job, and the arrangement on the job is that in twenty weeks, I'm to hand you the script. That's what the

58 *Killin' Generals*

contract says. It doesn't say I'm an employee. I'm a contractor. I found out through working with Zanuck that I can make more speed and more time this way. If I finish the thing, then we can go to work on it, or you can go to work on it, all you want. But if I have to stop every two or three weeks for you to examine things, to talk about things, Christ, I could be forty weeks doing this, because I could get upset and say, "Christ, I've got to rewrite this now and start over,'" and all that kind of stuff.

"Kenny didn't understand that, at first. He never worked with anybody like that. I said, 'I suppose we can drop it, because that's the only way I can do it.' Then his father, Eliot, whom I knew, called and said, 'What's this routine with you and Kenny?' I explained it to him and he understood at once. He said, 'All right, forget it. I'll tell Kenny, and you work exactly the way you've always worked. Wouldn't dream of asking you to work differently.' So that's the way it was done."

Johnson, back in England, began working on the script for *The Dirty Dozen* in May 1965, with the book to be published the same month. "In the beginning, Nunnally Johnson . . . wrote to me from England," recalled Nathanson. "He asked if I [would like] to work with him. I said, 'Yes, I'd love to! But did you know I've already written one screenplay for the film?' He wrote back, 'No, nobody ever tells the writer anything.' That was the end of it. He suggested I have my agent or lawyer get in touch with the film people, whoever was in charge, about getting me the assignment to work with him."

While Johnson labored on the script, Hyman was busy scouting for a director and the cast. He had only one director in mind, but when asked whether he would consider a backup choice if that director wasn't available or interested, he came up with a possible alternative thanks to a screening of *The Hill* at Cannes. "This guy had come up to me after the screening and said, 'That was a helluva film.' I said, 'Thank you. That's very nice of you. Who are you?' He said, 'My name is Peckinpah.' I said, 'Nice to meet you, Mr. Peckinpah.' When I left Cannes, I screened *Ride the High Country* [1962], and I was knocked out by Peckinpah's work."

The two men's paths would cross again a few years later in an even greater capacity, but it's interesting to consider how *The Dirty Dozen* may have turned out had Hyman's first choice not panned out. However, that director was indeed available, and quite eager to work on the project. His name was Robert Aldrich.

Aldrich was a logical choice for Hyman, as they'd worked together previously on the wildly successful *Baby Jane*, which Hyman had set up at Warner Bros. Consequently, Hyman was also very familiar with the director's reputation for being a straight-talking, no-holds-barred maverick—what is often termed in the industry as "difficult." As Aldrich himself would later say, "Most of the time people think I'm a son of a bitch, but I know exactly what I'm doing, and I know my job—most of the time, but not all the time."

Aldrich's reputation was well-earned. Born August 9, 1918, into a well-respected financial and political dynasty in Rhode Island (Nelson Rockefeller was his cousin), Aldrich immediately disdained the trappings of his ancestry. Performing well in college as a business major, he also excelled in football. A knee injury on the gridiron ended those aspirations, but when an uncle offered to get him a job at RKO Pictures, the stocky young man eagerly took him up on the offer. His family having disinherited him, Aldrich worked his way up the studio ladder one carefully placed step at a time, absorbing every political and creative aspect of filmmaking as he went.

From 1941 on, Aldrich took every job available, learning

the business from the likes of such mentors as Orson Welles, Jean Renoir, Charlie Chaplin, William A. Wellman, and others. In 1953, after having been an assistant director to those men, he directed his first film. He eventually earned acclaim in Europe and criticism in the US for the 1955 potboiler *Kiss Me Deadly*, starring Ralph Meeker as Mickey Spillane's detective Mike Hammer. The parable of nuclear annihilation added to the story had American critics scratching their heads as they complained about the violence. In Europe, as with cult directors Don Siegel and Sam Fuller, Aldrich was hailed as a new auteur. The controversy of Aldrich's films would be a hallmark of his career.

Over the next decade, directing work in both film and TV followed. When he had a say over the material, Aldrich folded prominent themes of redemption and retaining self-respect into the projects. Films such as *Apache* (1954), *Vera Cruz* (1954), *The Big Knife* (1955), *Attack!* (1956), *The Last Sunset* (1961), and others concealed these themes in anti-authority messages in the midst of complicated plots. By the time he made the gothic Bette Davis thrillers *What Ever Happened to Baby Jane?* and *Hush . . . Hush, Sweet Charlotte* (1964), he was at the top of his game. Following his criminally underrated yet taut thriller *The Flight of the Phoenix* (1965), Ken Hyman approached him to direct *The Dirty Dozen*.

Aldrich was very familiar with the project, as he had tried to option it himself when it was still in galley form but was outbid by MGM. He was eager to tackle it but objected to some of the things Hyman had done, such as approaching John Wayne to play the lead role of John Reisman. Luckily for Aldrich, Wayne had read the material and sent MGM the following response: "I have the premonition that whoever wrote this, if still in school, would be wearing sandals and carrying

MOST MISERABLE SON OF A BITCH

signs against the war in Vietnam, and would have an utter lack of respect for the men who fight their battles for them." Interestingly put, as the screenwriter was sixty-six years old.

John Wayne's rejection of *The Dirty Dozen* wasn't the only problem Aldrich had with the project. He had read Nunnally Johnson's finished draft, and in a January 1966 memo to Hyman, he wrote: "What we have now is a good script, in many instances a fine script. In many instances a great script, but it has a 1940s flavor and a 1950 point of view. We're talking about cancer, not ice cream, because today, war is cancer."

That said, he would go on in the same lengthy memo to detail why changes should be made to the existing script: "You see, what we have on our hands is the absolutely unique, never seen before, never to be seen again, opportunity of having our cake and eating it too. It's all there, all waiting to be taken. All we have to do is to think a little, and then take it. And again, in an effort to avoid abrasion and seek cohesion, let me anticipate your immediate reaction of 'But, Bob, you said you liked the script.' Allow me to answer with yes, I did and yes, I do, but it could be even better. It must be better. If you choose to press the point, I would have to reply that you too deceived me in agreeing to hire Wayne without my approval, but that's yesterday's news. What about today's news and tomorrow's promise? I'm sure there are good and valid reasons why a month has gone by without new pages that have to do with how we set up this story. Whatever those reasons are I can't accept the burden of making them my reasons, so let me restate on broad general terms what the problems are as I see them and how the attitudes and perspectives of the script have to be changed; then, let's talk specifically of the changes required."

He proceeded to do just that further on in the same memo. Zeroing in on one particular aspect of the main character, he emphatically said: "Reisman has to be the most cynical, suspicious, sophisticated, antiauthoritarian, antiestablishment, mean, miserable son of a bitch that anyone has ever seen in a movie. His estimation of his own character would be that it only has two flaws: an irrepressible sense of humor and an unremovable love for his fellow man, both of which he considers weaknesses. And humor. Whatever happened to the humor? If there was a script that called for, begged for, yearned for, *Dirty Dozen* is that script. Reisman is the most nonconformist, singularly smug, self-righteous, self-assured, cocky, conceited bastard that ever got bypassed by lesser men." In essence, he was describing himself.

He would go on for twelve more pages, meticulously describing the characters and how they needed to be improved upon. To drive the point home, Aldrich and Hyman agreed to bring in Aldrich's own often-used writer from his stable of creators. Writer Lukas Heller would do many rewrites during the month of April, as he had on several previous and future Aldrich projects. Born on July 21, 1930, Heller came from a prominent Jewish family in Germany and started his screenwriting career in Britain in the late 1950s. He wrote several low-budget dramatic scripts, first for television and then for feature films. Arriving in Hollywood in 1962, he teamed up with Aldrich on six films, sharing the Edgar Allan Poe Award for Best Motion Picture Screenplay with *Hush . . . Hush, Sweet Charlotte*'s original author, Henry Farrell. When Heller came to work on *The Dirty Dozen*, it would result in all hell breaking loose, especially in the eyes of Nunnally Johnson.

PART II

Production

5

DAPPER DAN
AND LADY TIGHT-GUTS

The script for *The Dirty Dozen* is best described as loosely based on Nathanson's novel, as much was changed or compacted, including both plot and characters. Writer Lukas Heller would also revise and edit Nunnally Johnson's work. There are more than eight different revisions of the script, dating back to May 1964. Most of those changes were made in April 1966, but significant alterations were performed from the outset. For example, John Reisman is a major instead of a captain, and he's regular army, not OSS. "This is not an army mission," Nathanson said. "The movie glossed over all that. They made it seem like army command did the whole thing. In the novel, in going over my research, I made it OSS. The OSS would have done it, and did do things like that." Also, during WWII the army was still segregated, and the likes of Napoleon White would not have been one of the dozen.

In terms of the dozen themselves, several characters were morphed into one. Archer Maggott was still a redneck bigot, but since he was also made a religious fanatic and a sexual psychopath, both Myron Odell and Calvin Ezra Smith were no longer in the story. Instead, the dozen were rounded out with Milo Vladek and Tassos Bravos.

The script also gives capsule descriptions of the major characters. Reisman is described as being a tough, forty-year-old professional soldier from Virginia, not Chicago. Making him a Virginian makes sense when he says to Maggott, "We southern boys have to stick together."

The officers Reisman meets with early on are given rather sardonic descriptions. General Worden is described as a tough professional with rough edges, looking like he just gave up chewing tobacco. General Denton is a smooth and sophisticated one-star general whose cunning and ambition will probably earn him more. Captain Kinder is a dark young man of obvious intellect, and Major Max Armbruster is a mild-mannered, scholarly looking soldier. Colonel Everett Dasher Breed, the obvious antagonist to Reisman, is considered an immaculately tailored product of West Point, not unlike something out of *Madame Butterfly*. The facade serves to disguise an efficient and consumingly ambitious career officer.

In the sequence in which Reisman meets the dozen, those characters are summarized with a bit more detail. First is Victor Franko, a Chicago hoodlum who has already spent ten years in various penitentiaries. Next is Robert Jefferson (Napoleon White in the novel), dubbed a huge, intelligent Black man. Maggott is said to be a redneck from the Bible Belt whose only achievement in life has been graduating from his rural, cracker background to the seamy streets of Phenix City, Alabama, across the bridge from Fort Benning in Georgia. He maintains that he went there to spread the word of the Lord and preach against the influence of Blacks, Catholics, Jews, and anyone else who didn't subscribe to his particular form of religious mania. Since he was convicted of murder and rape, he obviously found Phenix City interesting for other than religious reasons.

The other prisoners given more detail include Samson Posey, a part Native American giant with little formal education. Joseph Wladislaw is said to be a granite-faced but not unintelligent man who was an officer at the time of his court-martial. Pedro Jiminez is a boyishly handsome Mexican whose amiable manner can quickly turn reckless and hot-tempered.

The remaining members of the dozen are Tassos Bravos, a little man of high intelligence who seems out of place among the others; Seth Sawyer, the only other prisoner who had been in combat; wily stick-up man Roscoe Lever; the violent-looking Milo Vladek, capable of anything and sentenced to a long term for desertion; and Vernon Pinkley, who's described as having a sad, bloodhound face.

The other characters with descriptions are Clyde Bowren and Carl Morgan, who are both guards but with ranks different from those in the novel. Morgan is a rather sly and aggressive corporal, while Sergeant Bowren is an open-faced yet frighteningly tough MP.

Much of the dialogue following the introduction of the characters is very much like that in the finished film, with only slight differences that most likely come from the polish provided later by Lukas Heller. The script includes the character of Lady Margot Strathallan, whom Johnson describes as a beautifully formed thirty-five-year-old whose bearing and upbringing make her tantalizing and attractive. She is always aware of being a lady but is a woman only in moments of intimacy. She and Reisman tangle from the start.

After the camp is set up, the exhausted men sleep in their unfinished barracks, not pup tents as in the book. Jiminez, who now has strings for his guitar, strums along to the woman on the radio singing "Lili Marlene." Special lyrics are added at the end of the script for Wladislaw to sing, and the others join in. The next day is the training scene with Jiminez halfway up a suspended rope, too frightened to climb all the way up. The scene was written to take place on a beach cliff and not a free-standing tower, but the result is the same.

The next scene in the script (which was cut from the film) has Captain Kinder discussing the results of the inkblot tests he gave the men with Reisman. Pinkley saw an old man trying to drown his wife's cat; Maggott saw a woman chained in a cellar. Kinder then says Wladislaw saw General MacArthur with a sack on his head, and Sawyer simply sat trembling until Kinder took the inkblot away.

As the two men discuss the results of the tests and Reisman says the men will not be replaced, they hear a commotion outside: Lady Margot has come into the camp. Reisman politely yet firmly reminds her the compound is off-limits. She mentions that Colonel Breed must be Reisman's commanding officer; Reisman disguises his surprise but is adamant about her leaving. After Bowren escorts Lady Margot out, Reisman shares his suspicion with Kinder, telling him, "If I know anything, we've just stumbled on a real old-fashioned romance. Old Dapper Dan and the recently bereaved Lady Tight-Guts. He'd throw the war for a wife with a title."

Kinder asks Reisman what gives between him and Breed. Reisman explains that he was under Breed's command in Sicily and disobeyed Breed's orders to put on a show of explosives for a visiting general. He adds that it might have cost half the company and not really meant anything to Breed. Returning to the subject of Lady Margot, Reisman tells Kinder she was obviously doing some spying for Breed.

As he lights cigarettes for himself and Kinder, Reisman notices something above him and excuses himself for a moment. Maggott has been on guard duty in the watchtower, and although he has no ammo, he uses the rifle sights to aim at Kinder and mutter to himself what he would do if he had ammo. Suddenly, the rifle is snatched from his grip and the butt is brought down hard on the back of Maggott's head, knocking him unconscious. From the watchtower Reisman calls the prisoners out and tells them it will be healthier for them to not do what he caught Maggott doing when on guard duty.

As in the finished film, the next scene in the script is the dozen's refusal to shave, but this time Posey is the last holdout, not Maggott. Following that comes a scene that wasn't used in the film showing several of the dozen playing poker for cigarettes. Posey deals and catches Maggott cheating by raising him to his feet after he wins a hand, making the cards he'd stashed behind his knees fall to the floor. Reisman, Bowren, and Kinder enter just as Posey is about to punch the preaching Maggott. Reisman has the cigarettes redistributed and proceeds to describe the night's exercise.

Jefferson and Wladislaw are to each lead a group with specific orders to not be detected as they attempt to capture the other based on Reisman's rules and with no guards in attendance. As the men leave, Reisman calls Wladislaw aside and asks him if he thinks the men can be trusted. He says no, begins to leave, stops, and adds, "Not yet."

While the men are out on the exercise, Reisman sees a light flicker briefly at the manor house. He tells Kinder he thinks the bereaved widow has a visitor. When the men return, they're exhausted from the exercise, which is deemed a success despite what Reisman calls a few "irregularities." When the men hit the sack, Wladislaw asks Jefferson what

Reisman meant, and Jefferson explains that he put Franko and Maggott under arrest in a nearby truck for trying to foul up the exercise. In the truck, Franko mutters to Maggott that he'll kill Reisman at the firing range the next day.

The truck Franko and Maggott are in is parked under guard near the manor house, and Reisman decides to confirm his suspicions about Lady Margot by walking over and casually chatting with the truck driver. He discovers from the driver that Breed has been making regular nocturnal visits for the last six months. Franko tries to hear the conversation but is sent to the rear of the truck by the guard. Reisman returns to the encampment to tell Kinder that Breed's been visiting Lady Margot for the last six months, but her husband was determined to be KIA only six weeks ago. Amused, Kinder says Breed is guilty of conduct unbecoming an officer. At the same time, Maggott informs Franko that if one releases the safety on a grease gun and simply bumps it, it will fire nonstop. Franko is impressed.

At the rifle range the next day, Maggott, Franko, and Jiminez are first on the firing line. Reisman reminds Bowren about his saying that the first chance one of the dozen gets, he'll shoot the major in the head, and adds that this would be their chance. The men listen to Reisman's instructions as three plywood targets painted to look like Nazis spring up. Reisman stands between the targets and the firing line to pass out the ammo as Kinder, Bowren, and two other MPs watch nervously. Jiminez fumbles with his submachine gun as Franko and Maggott stand ready to fire. Reisman walks to the target pit with his back to the men, never looking behind him. Franko takes off the safety and turns slightly sideways, ready to shoot, as Jiminez finally loads his weapon.

When Bowren blows his whistle to commence firing, no one does, as they're all watching Franko intently. Bowren shouts at the men to fire, and slowly all three shoot. The targets disintegrate in a hail of bullets. A slow smile grows on Franko's face as he realizes that he can kill Reisman when the time is right for him.

On the march back to the compound Maggott grumbles about marching twenty-five miles on foot while the officers and guards travel by truck. However, once they reach the compound, they see that a field kitchen has been set up with hot food to be served for the first time in weeks. Reisman says they start jump school in two days, then tells Kinder privately that he doesn't want Breed to give him trouble, calling him "a sweet-smelling, jumped-up West Point tailor's dummy."

At Breed's jump school, the scene plays out as it does in the film, with very minor changes. Pinkley, acting as a general, inspects the troops, and later Wladislaw is beaten by several of Breed's men, which the rest of the dozen believe is Reisman's doing.

In between those scenes, Reisman is purposely humiliated in front of everyone by Breed. As Reisman prepares to jump, he pushes off from the jump tower. Breed takes over the loudspeaker and asks if Reisman is ready. Reisman is kept dangling as Breed keeps asking Reisman to speak up. Breed continues to keep Reisman dangling until the mechanism finally releases him and he makes a perfect landing.

On the ground, Reisman asks Posey and Jiminez if he could be heard, and they say perfectly well. All the dozen saw and heard what happened, and they join Reisman in his hatred of Breed. Reisman gets the others out of earshot, turns off Breed's loudspeaker, and confronts him angrily. Breed smiles and says Reisman is guilty of insubordination. Reisman stands his ground.

The next day Reisman, Bowren, and the dozen are in a C-47

transport plane, ready to make a real jump. Reisman is first, followed by Maggott, Franko, and Bowren. As Reisman stands in the open doorway waiting for the signal, Franko makes a gesture with his thumb and forefinger as if he's going to unhook Reisman's chute before he jumps. He turns his head to smile at the dozen but sees instead an unsmiling Bowren. Following this scene in the film, stock footage of fourteen parachutes floating successfully to the ground is shown.

The next night, the dozen are enjoying a rare rest period as Maggott stands guard duty in the watchtower. Several of the men listen to Jiminez playing his guitar to a song not yet written but that will be "The Bramble Bush" in the film. (The song would later be released as a single and go to number four on the adult contemporary chart.) Reisman talks briefly to Morgan and then departs as a truck backs into the compound. What then plays out is the prostitute sequence seen in the film.

The main addition to this moment is Reisman and Kinder saying how well the men are doing, save for Maggott, and that maybe they should have invited Breed and Denton to the party. Maggott follows the same path Reisman took when he jumped Maggott in the watchtower previously, muttering to himself about how Reisman is spitting in the face of "the Redeemer." In the hut, Pinkley tells Bravos he sees only eight women for the dozen; Bravos responds, "You just noticed that?" Simultaneously, Maggott creeps up behind Reisman, ready to strike him with a metal bar he found. Knowing he's there, Reisman wheels around and flips Maggott over his shoulder, karate chopping him when he rises again. Reisman looks down at Maggott sprawled in the dirt and says, "You just haven't learned a thing, have you?"

In the hut, several of the dozen are drunkenly teaching some of the women their own version of "Lili Marlene." A female scream comes from off-screen, announcing her dress is ripped. She then runs into the compound giggling as Posey lumbers after her. Franko asks Wladislaw if he thinks Posey needs help, and Wladislaw says, "Don't worry. He'll figure it out."

The next morning, Morgan, who has no idea what happened the previous evening, stands guard at the gate as two trucks pull up. A squadron of Breed's paratroopers tumbles out, followed by Breed himself, who commands the gate be opened. Morgan sees three paratroopers move in support of Breed, two of whom were part of the group that beat Wladislaw. Bowren approaches and sees Morgan doing whatever Breed asks. Breed's men disarm Bowren and the rest of the guards as Breed interrogates Morgan, but luckily he knows nothing. The dozen have gathered by this point and see everything.

Driving up outside the compound, Reisman sees the trucks and sneaks out of his jeep. Breed has the dozen fall in as Jefferson and Posey notice the men who attacked Wladislaw. Breed goes down the line and stops at "General" Pinkley. Franko speaks out, and Breed orders him to shave. When he refuses, three of Breed's men grab him in an attempt to force him to do so. As Franko struggles, Posey, Jefferson, and Wladislaw jump the men holding Franko and wrestle them to the ground.

The rest of the dozen break ranks and prepare to fight when a machine gun bursts from the top of the hut and everyone hits the dirt, including Breed. Reisman fires several more bursts as Breed's men heed Reisman's orders to surrender their weapons. The dozen help Bowren gather the weapons as Reisman comes down from the roof and asks Breed to talk in his office.

Still holding him at gunpoint, Reisman tells the seated Breed he's in trouble for trespassing in a maximum-security area. Breed counters by mentioning the prostitutes. Reisman says he doesn't have to ask where that info came from, to which

Breed responds that it was Morgan. Reisman wisecracks that none of the prostitutes were widows, or at least not "recent" widows. When Breed asks him to explain that remark, Reisman says he believes it's not necessary to explain it.

Later, in General Denton's office, General Worden, Col. Breed, and Maj. Armbruster sit in stony silence as Denton reads Reisman the riot act. Reisman seriously considers bringing up Lady Margot and Breed, but instead contends that his men are better than Breed's "chocolate soldiers." Told by Denton not to be abusive and to prove his statement, Reisman is about to bring up Lady Margot when he's stopped by Armbruster, who mentions the planned war games. Reisman picks up on it and volunteers his men against Breed's. All agree they would like to see that.

The opening scene from the war games then plays out as in the film, but in the script the arriving (no longer dirty) dozen all sing their private version of "Lili Marlene." The script then contains a scene of Reisman and Denton at headquarters, trading barbs and quips as they await radio news about the war game. In the field, Franko prevents a guard from seeing several of the dozen hiding in some bushes by donning an umpire's helmet and telling the guard he just stepped on an anti-personnel device. Franko takes his weapon and tells the man to return to the unit on the double and report himself dead.

Prior to the fake jeep accident scenario, Wladislaw shows Armbruster, who's acting as an observer, the live timed pencil explosives, which he then gives to Jefferson in case they're needed for "Plan B." Later, Gilpin puts the timed pencil explosives into the removed boots of the "wounded" Posey. Before the ambulance arrives, Wladislaw slowly slides the boots under the radio table and keeps nervously checking his watch. When Breed is captured, Wladislaw tells Gilpin he has exactly forty-five seconds to defuse the explosives. In the finished film, however, the timed pencil explosives are shown but never explained.

At headquarters, Denton hears the announcement of Breed's capture and disputes it when he discovers that the dozen broke the rules, especially in switching armbands and destroying the jeep. A prolonged argument ensues between Denton and Reisman about Reisman's future as an officer and the dozen being sent back to prison. It becomes a three-way shouting match when Breed joins in. General Worden enters the office and asks the premise of the discussion; he's told by Denton that Reisman's mission should be canceled due to the dozen's behavior in the war games. Worden not only disagrees but, having witnessed it himself, calls it the best tactical exercise he's seen in a long, long time, proving that Reisman and his men might just pull off the mission.

Reisman, Bowren, and the dozen have a celebratory dinner back at the compound, during which the men serenade Reisman with their version of "Lili Marlene" which he hadn't heard before. After a few jokes, Reisman proceeds to go through the plan for the mission with a pointer and a model of the château. When a toy car indicating Reisman, Wladislaw, and Pinkley is shown, Franko sees the figure of a milkmaid in the car and asks which one is the major.

Otherwise, the scene plays out as in the film, cutting to the men and Reisman on the C-47 ready to jump. Reisman keeps his eyes on Maggott, not knowing what to expect, when Bravos asks how much longer the flight will be. Reisman gets up to check and sees Bowren, who has stowed away in a cargo space. When Reisman asks, Bowren says he's there to ensure Maggott doesn't flip out. He confirms that he has a parachute.

The remainder of the script, despite its many revisions, plays out almost exactly as the film does, with Jiminez still very much a part of the entire mission. It's mentioned that Maggott has his own plans and even pulls up the rope to the château to keep the others from coming up until Jefferson stops him. Just prior to Maggott's murder of the German girl, the script calls for a "Director's Sequence," in which the events of the next few minutes will happen so fast that it will be confusing to read.

There are only a few other significant differences between the script and the finished film: first, Smith is still mentioned as one of the dozen, and second, in Posey's final scene, Bravos lies dying beside him as Posey keeps firing the heavy machine gun until he hears voices moving in. Badly wounded now, he slumps over his empty machine gun. He then drags himself to his knees, pulls the pin on a grenade, throws it, and hears screams behind him when it explodes. He smiles and drags himself into the underbrush.

The mission completed, General Worden, not Armbruster, provides the final voice-over recounting the success of the mission and that Sawyer and Posey were wounded and captured but subsequently liberated. Worden and Denton visit Bowren, Reisman, and Wladislaw in the hospital, with the generals telling them patronizingly what a fine job they did. Wladislaw is simply described as being the same unrepentant rebel he's always been.

Nunnally Johnson's script, revised several times by Lukas Heller, met with Robert Aldrich's satisfaction, and he and Ken Hyman proceeded to line up a cast. Not satisfied, however, were the good people in charge of enforcing the Motion Picture Production Code.

6

"IT WAS AN INTERESTING AND TENUOUS TIME"

The version of the script described in the previous chapter still needed to pass muster with the Motion Picture Production Code and its 1960s version of moral protocols. Geoffrey Shurlock had taken over as administrator in 1954 from the ailing and notorious Joseph Breen. Due to cultural changes, such as television and the importing of foreign films into the country, Shurlock had taken a more lenient approach toward censorship than Breen did.

However, Shurlock still took issue with the language, and that required changes. As he wrote in this 1965 letter to the head of MGM, "While certain profanity, particularly in the use of 'hell' and 'damn' are sometimes in a limited quantity acceptable to the plot, motivation, or authentic characterization, the repeated casual use of this type of language becomes offensive and unacceptable." He later added in the same letter, he did "not approve of 'God damn, son of a bitch, bastard,' vulgar slang references to excrement, and the male sex organ. . . . Seriously urge you to reconsider derogatory 'nigger, wop, dago, jew.'"

In the earliest version of Nunnally Johnson's script, he apparently included a scene of John Reisman having a casual affair with the barmaid Tess. Shurlock adamantly stated, "Unacceptable casual presentation of the sexual relationship between Reisman and Tessie, particularly in the beginning of the scene in her room. The beginning of the scene would indicate that he had slept with her the night before, and the scene terminates when apparently 'flattening her again.'"

The executives at MGM sought to appease Shurlock's requests throughout 1965 and into 1966 with a series of inter-office memos that also included input from director Robert Aldrich. In April 1966 Aldrich sent a letter to the MPA (renamed the MPAA in 1968) and cc'ed a copy to Ken Hyman in which he attempted to end the rancor that had been brewing over the scene and language issues. In referring to the requested changes, he wrote: "Air-expressed copies of *The Dirty Dozen*. I have taken the liberty of doing this directly instead of through Ken Hyman in order to expedite any problems that may arise, though none are anticipated." It certainly helped, but apparently not enough, as Shurlock wrote back, "Better but . . . Goddamn, still a problem. Eight bastards and eight bastards are too many."

Shurlock also took umbrage with the scene (written similarly to the version in the novel) in which Reisman brings in a prostitute for all the men. For some strange reason, when the one prostitute was changed to several, Shurlock was appeased. According to author Nathanson, Aldrich was being much more charitable to the dozen than he was in his book.

Aldrich let it be known that it was too late to make the other major requested script changes, since filming was set to start the following week, on April 25, 1966. Shurlock suggested, "Consider a protection shot to cover this dialogue ['wop bastard,'] and 'nigger' . . . can be acceptable or unacceptable depending on the situation and who uses them." The practice of shooting scenes more than once with different dialogue as protection was a practice that had begun at that time and that's still in use to this day when a film is to be shown on network TV. In early May Aldrich simply wrote back, "Okay, okay. So it won't be 'wop bastard.' Alright? Warmest regards, Robert Aldrich."

The censorship battle dealt with, Aldrich and Hyman still had other issues to handle. Aldrich's hiring of Lukas Heller to punch up Johnson's script was met with great disdain by Johnson. It wasn't so much any individual scene changes that bothered Johnson; his ire was raised by the very fact that Aldrich brought in another writer at all. The then sexagenarian Georgia native was a veteran of over fifty film screenplays, and had rarely if ever shared screen credit with another writer.

Despite his age, he understood the requirements of the script in light of the escalation of the Vietnam War. "War is a dreadful thing," he said years later. "If people are going to be killed and their bones broken and their heads busted open, you have to go along with that." The Gulf of Tonkin Incident resulted in the passage of the Gulf of Tonkin Resolution in Congress, giving President Lyndon Johnson much broader authority to escalate the war than ever before. At the time Nunnally Johnson submitted his first draft of the script for *The Dirty Dozen*, troop levels had increased to 184,000, and the war's popularity waned with its escalation.

Aldrich's reasoning for bringing in Heller was that "Metro must have had three hundred thousand dollars tied up in aborted *Dirty Dozen* scripts by then, and I wanted a whole new concept. Well, despite considerable resistance, we got a whole new concept." In the same interview he concluded, "With the *Dozen*, two things happened. One, Heller and I stumbled onto the dissatisfaction, particularly on the part of the younger public, with the establishment. I'd like to say we anticipated that kind of success, but we didn't, really. If you read the book, however, that kind of antiauthoritarian attitude, that point of view, isn't there; and Heller did an excellent screenplay. So we got on a wave that we never knew was coming—not a wave, a tidal wave. But we didn't see it forming."

For Lukas Heller's part, he was simply the go-to guy Aldrich preferred when it came to rewrites or adaptations. The German-born Heller had started in television in the late 1950s but was chosen by Aldrich to adapt screenplays for *What Ever Happened to Baby Jane?*, *Hush . . . Hush, Sweet Charlotte*, and *The Flight of the Phoenix*. Like most successful directors, Aldrich preferred to work with the same creative entities on a project, such as Heller, composer Frank De Vol, and film editor Michael Luciano, all of whom worked on *The Dirty Dozen*.

According to Heller in a 1986 interview, "Aldrich was offered the movie and said he would do it on the condition that I rewrite it, which the producer objected to violently— not so much . . . because he objected to me but because he felt I was being forced down his throat." He went on to say, "There was a great deal of dissension about that movie. Ken Hyman was mad at me, partly because he couldn't quite stand up to Aldrich, couldn't deal with Aldrich, and I was a good scapegoat." Asked recently about this statement, Ken Hyman responded, "I don't know what the hell he's talking about. Lukas Heller, I don't think I met him more than once. He was somebody I did not know and I really was not excited about knowing him. He reworked Nunnally Johnson's script in concert with Bob Aldrich." Heller's take on the matter may never be known, as he died in England in 1988 at the age of fifty-eight.

None of this mattered to Johnson, who contacted first Ken Hyman and then ultimately the Writer's Guild of America to state his case for earning a lone writing credit. Johnson had been one of the founders of the Guild and relied on their judgment. The arbitration resulted in co-credit for Johnson and Heller, which Johnson despised, saying publicly he had been fired for the first time in his life. He later gave this as the reason why he never saw the finished film: "It was like the expectant father getting intimations that he isn't the father of the baby, so he doesn't look forward to the birth with great excitement." Several false starts followed, but *The Dirty Dozen* would be Johnson's last filmed screenplay. He died in 1977.

The script revisions, in light of both censorship issues and battling writer credits, were ongoing as Hyman and Aldrich attempted to cobble together a worthy cast. Aldrich was pleased that John Wayne had passed on playing Reisman, saying, "I'm a Wayne fan. His politics don't bother me; that's his mother's problem. But not Wayne for the part."

Other actors, such as Burt Lancaster, George Chakiris, and Aldo Ray, had been approached for various roles by Hyman before Aldrich came on board.

None of them were cast, but most interesting of all was Jack Palance, who had worked with Aldrich in several previous films. It had been announced in *Variety* that he was to play Maggott, but no contract had yet been signed. He was to be paid $125,000 plus $1,000 a week for sixteen weeks. Palance not only turned down the part, he made the announcement during a curtain speech in Anaheim on the last day of the play he had been appearing in, while also denigrating Anaheim itself. He said playing Maggott would have required him to hate based on the color of another actor's skin, stressing, "We don't need to make pictures showing how nasty the whites are to Negroes." His onstage speech included the work he had personally done to advance Black people in the film industry and then asked why he was "sent to a stinking place like Anaheim" before leaving the stage.

Luckily for Hyman, the choice Aldrich had in mind from the beginning to play John Reisman, Lee Marvin, was available. They met with him on location in the Nevada desert, where he was filming *The Professionals* (1966). Hyman jokingly reminded the actor that they had both been in the Marines, but since the actor was a private and Hyman a corporal, he was outranked and would have taken orders from Hyman.

Actually, Lee Marvin's association with violence began long before his experiences in the Marines. An overview of his ancestry shows a legacy of noble achievements tinged with violence. The actor was aware of his family history and often joked that he was the charcoal gray sheep of a family that first came to America as Puritans. Matthew Marvin was a Puritan leader who forcefully dragged his followers out of taverns on Sundays. Lee's father lost both his parents at an early age and was taken in by his uncle Ross Marvin, a Cornell professor and Arctic explorer. It isn't widely known, but Ross Marvin died during Admiral Peary's 1908–9 expedition to the North Pole, a victim of homicide.

Lee came into the world on February 19, 1924, a year and a half after his brother, Robert. His parents were WWI veteran Lamont "Monte" Marvin and Virginia native Courtenay Washington Davidge. Both parents drank excessively, leading to alcohol-fueled fights that progressed into abusive behavior as Lee and Robert grew older.

Lee's parents decided to enroll him at St. Leo's College

Preparatory School in Florida, where he quickly endeared himself to the all-boys campus by breaking state records in the jave-
lin and high hurdles. He sometimes ran afoul of the faculty—all
brothers of the Order of Saint Benedict—by slaughtering a
wild boar with a handmade spear, making alcohol in his dorm
room, and invading a nearby Catholic girls' school. Despite
these antics, the young man with the booming voice was well-
liked by the faculty. As Fr. James Hoge joked when Lee was
awarded an honorary doctorate in 1969, "Lee Marvin was not
the worst student I had, and certainly was not the best. He was
the damnedest student I ever had."

Following the attack on Pearl Harbor, Lee received his
father's permission to drop out and join the Marines at age
seventeen. He eventually became a top-flight Marine trained
in explosives, and later an impressive scout sniper. Lee was
seriously wounded during a firefight on Saipan, which resulted
in his being sent home thirteen months later with a nearly
severed sciatic nerve. He wrote his father about it shortly after
it happened:

7/3/44: Dear Pop;

I am writing you this letter mostly to tell you that I am
really all right and that things are not as bad as they
seem. I was on Saipan when I got hit. Not too bad but
bad enough to hamper me if I stayed. I was hit in my left
buttocks just below the belt line.

You may think it's funny to get hit in the can like
that but at the time I was very lucky that that is all I
got. I was pinned down and could not move an inch and
then a sniper started on me. His first shot hit my foot
and his second was just about three inches in front of
my nose. It was just a matter of time, as I knew I would

get hit sooner or later. If I got up and ran I would not be writing this letter so I just kept down. I could see nothing to fire at so there I was.

Bang! It felt like someone hit me with a 2 × 4. The wound starts about ¼" from my spine on a slight forward angle where it left the flesh. It was a sniper that hit me and he must have been using a flat nose slug, as it did not leave two little holes. It entered about ½" where it did and just laid it all open. Now there is more or less a gash 8" long by 3" wide and about 2" deep. It did not touch the muscle or spine at all. Geez, now you have never seen creeping like I did but he kept on shooting. Finally, I got out of there and I am OK now. I am now on Guadalcanal and awaiting transfer south. They figure on letting the wound fill in so that will take about 4 or 5 months. They gave me the Purple Heart and all the trimmings but I still think that it was worth it.

The guilt Lee Marvin suffered while the rest of his comrades continued to fight and die remained with him for the rest of his life. It also resulted in a lifelong battle with PTSD, resulting in such symptoms as alcoholism, a constant need for violence, and screaming nightmares.

The Marvin family was more dysfunctional than ever following Monte's army discharge. Monte had envied his two sons (Robert served in the Army Air Forces) and had reenlisted at age forty-one, minus his commission. Upon returning home, he found the adjustment so traumatic that he attempted suicide. During Monte's recuperation, the family settled in Woodstock, New York, where Lee found therapeutic work as a plumber's apprentice.

Life in Woodstock for Lee consisted of drinks with the local artisans, fights with his family, and nightmares of reliving the war. His struggles eventually found an outlet in a local theater group. He later said, "Summer stock was the closest thing to the Marine Corps way of life I could find—hard work and no crap." After summer stock, Lee enrolled in the American Theatre Wing under the GI Bill. It was a perfect venue for him, since it was established to train returning vets in the arts and, as Lee would later recall, "All the guys were vets, and we all knew each other's problems. It was marvelous."

Lee pounded the pavement looking for work, and did surprisingly well for a young, gangly, unhandsome actor, getting regular gigs in live theater, television, and military training films. During this time a friend asked him why he was constantly sporting new bruises, and Lee admitted to going into bars and purposely starting fights, but only when he knew he was outnumbered. His reasons were simple: The Marines taught him to kill, and this was the only way he could deal with the need for it without causing harm to anyone else. Unconsciously, Lee had diagnosed himself with posttraumatic stress disorder. An inability to confine his capacity for violence strictly to acting would haunt him for the rest of his life.

Following a minor role in the Broadway play *Billy Budd*, Marvin finagled a role as an extra in a Gary Cooper service comedy titled *You're in the Navy Now* (1951). When fledgling agent Meyer Mishkin got Marvin a few lines in the film, Lee agreed to have Mishkin represent him. Thus began one of the most successful collaborations in film history.

Between 1952 and 1954, Lee appeared in fifteen films. In all these roles, he was either in uniform, breaking the law, handling weapons, or, in some cases, all three. Lee's first lead role is a good example of what he contributed to his films. *Eight Iron Men* (1952)—originally titled *The Dirty Dozen* (!)—was a modest WWII thriller in which a small squad is pinned down by an unseen sniper. Director Edward Dmytryk recalled that when a gun didn't work, the studio property experts were at a loss to fix it. Lee asked to give it a try. Thanks to the actor's unique knowledge of firearms, which he would utilize throughout his career, the gun was available for the next scene. Lee's harrowing experiences in the Marines also gave him the authority to show another actor how to play a death scene. Away from the cast and crew, he told the actor that actual death is not nearly as theatrical as he was playing it, and his advice gave greater authenticity to a run-of-the-mill production.

Lee's greatest on-screen impact during this period came in a one-two combo punch, something he would do several times in his career. *The Wild One* (1953), starring a brooding Marlon Brando and a garrulous Lee as rival gang leaders, started the biker-movie phenomenon of the 1950s and '60s. The second film to show off his ability was Fritz Lang's classic noir *The Big Heat* (1953). Lee played his role of a sadistic hood so convincingly—especially in one infamous scene in which he scalds girlfriend Gloria Grahame with a pot of boiling coffee—that *New York Times* critic Vincent Canby dubbed him "the Merchant of Menace." Lee was no longer just one of Hollywood's many men you love to hate. His realistic and frightening portrayal of violence had moved him to its front ranks.

Though he played bad guys during the day, Lee enjoyed the Hollywood party circuit by night. It was at one such party that he met UCLA music graduate Betty Ebeling, a former nanny to Joan Crawford's children. After several months of commuting between their apartments, Lee finally proposed: "I guess we'll have to get married, if that's okay with you." Betty's pregnancy helped her decide.

Lee's relationship with Betty proved to be a true partnership.

He relied on her opinion when considering scripts, which he continued to do even after the marriage ended. Lee's introduction of his wife to any social gathering was short and concise: "I want you to meet my best friend and toughest critic." The Marvins also wasted no time doing what most young couples did in the early 1950s by contributing to the baby boom. First child and only son Christopher (1952) was followed by Courtenay (1954), Cynthia (1956), and Claudia (1958). As his children matured, Lee's claustrophobia about domestic life coincided with an escalation of his drinking and even more erratic behavior. He would sometimes disappear for days on end, as he had done when he was a child. These factors were the first cracks in a relationship Lee genuinely tried to maintain.

Lee made twelve films from 1955 to 1957 that had a great impact on the film community, including John Sturges's *Bad Day at Black Rock* (1955) and Robert Aldrich's *Attack!* (1956). In Richard Fleischer's *Violent Saturday* (1955), his performance as a hood robbing a small-town bank had critic Judith Crist commenting when the film was rereleased a decade later, "A pity we had to waste ten years watching any number of 'stars' do ineptly what he had clearly mastered years ago."

By the time he made Budd Boetticher's now revered western *7 Men from Now* (1956), Lee's flair had the film's star and coproducer Randolph Scott suggesting to Boetticher, "Why don't you give the kid more lyrics?" Boetticher heartily agreed and created a death scene Lee enacted so impressively that the preview audience made the projectionist rerun the scene.

He was asked many times to do a series but always declined, until Meyer Mishkin convinced him of the medium's virtues and its financial rewards. *M Squad* premiered in 1957, a half-hour police procedural with Lee as tough Chicago detective Lt. Frank Ballinger. Marvin's poignant performance as Native

American war hero Ira Hayes in "The American," an episode of *Sunday Showcase*, is a standout. For the episode "People Need People" of *Alcoa Premiere*, his riveting portrait of a mentally disturbed veteran garnered him an Emmy nomination.

The screen persona of Lee Marvin began to jell in the early 1960s. By now he had developed the prematurely white hair and muscular facial features that would be his trademark in a belated ascent to major stardom. From 1960 to 1963, all of Lee Marvin's work would be with John Wayne and director John Ford, together or separately. During the filming of *The Man Who Shot Liberty Valance* (1962), all concerned lived in fear of Ford—except Lee Marvin. Ford often called him to the set with, "Lee, take the stage!" As Liberty Valance, an utterly amoral outlaw, he gave the most evil performance ever witnessed in a Ford film.

A 1964 remake of *The Killers*, meant to be the first made-for-TV movie, was deemed too violent and released in theaters instead, where it became a box-office smash. Having the main character quip something humorously macabre just before the violence commences is a conceit still used by filmmakers to this day. Lee Marvin's famous last line to Angie Dickinson before he kills her ("Lady, I just don't have the time") set the standard long before Clint Eastwood asked the bad guy to make his day.

Making *Ship of Fools* (1965), with its cargo of massive egos, was a gargantuan headache for director Stanley Kramer. But Lee, playing a bigoted, lecherous but ultimately tragic ballplayer, turned in a powerful performance that began the Oscar buzz early. During that production, Lee met a stand-in/extra named Michelle Triola while he was still with Betty. The affair between Lee and Michelle led to an uneasy alliance between Betty and Lee to keep the details of the relationship out of the tabloids.

The 1960s were a turbulent time in America, and the

schisms were both reflected in and added to by the films of the day. Lee's career kicked into high gear with a series of films that established him as a new film icon in the cinema of violence. His protagonists were more mature and world-weary, capable of extreme violence when provoked, and completely devoid of sentiment, and had backstories the audience may or may not have known about. Everything he had accomplished before formed the ingredients that coalesced into the first contemporary action hero. Helping that image was Lee's role as Major John Reisman.

As costar Jim Brown remembers, "Lee Marvin was brilliant and witty and cerebral. He would speak in riddles and crack up the crew. Lee was a nice man, a powerful actor, but he was hitting the bottle pretty hard that summer. He'd show up on the set some days still high, be weaving and slurring, saying, 'All right, you Dirty Dozen, line up.' An understanding man, Aldrich would tell Lee's friend Robert Phillips, or Lee's woman, Michelle, to take Lee home. . . . One day Lee asked me if I ever had any acting lessons. I said, 'No, but I've got the best acting teachers in the world. I've got you guys.' And I did. Marvin helped me. George Kennedy helped me. It doesn't get much better than that."

And then came Bronson. The second lead was offered to an actor who served an even longer apprenticeship than Marvin in film and television and whose backstory was just as intriguing. The current popularity of superhero movies doesn't take into account that there once was a near true-life superhero named Charles Bronson, who would go on to make immensely successful films well into his fifties. According to Adam Klugman, son of actor Jack Klugman, the two men worked as barkers in Atlantic City after the war. As Adam recalled: "My father said that Charlie had a kind of superhuman kind of strength. To demonstrate that, he told the following story. They were walking along the beach in Atlantic City and encountered a young woman who was crying. They didn't know why she was crying, so they stopped, and Charles Bronson asked the woman. She said, 'Well, I've been at the beach, recently been engaged. I came here and I dropped my diamond engagement ring in between these two rocks.'

"Okay. So, Charles Bronson says to my father, 'Look, I'm gonna push this rock, and when I push this rock, I want you to reach down and grab her engagement ring and give it to her.' My father says, 'What are you, fucking crazy? You can't move this rock, Charlie, because it's a rock! It's not gonna move.' So Charlie says, 'Just do it!' So, my father says, skeptically, 'Okay,' thinking that of course this is complete delusion on the part of Charlie Bronson, who, as strong as he is, is not going to be able to move a huge fucking rock that's sitting on the beach. So, Charlie Bronson leans up against this rock and begins pushing it. And, to my father's amazement, the rock moves. While Charlie is pushing the rock, my father reaches down and grabs this woman's engagement ring and gives it to her. He said that she was incredibly grateful and shocked. She [had been] as skeptical as my father that Charlie was actually going to be able to do this. But that is what happened, and my father swears that it's true."

Even before that remarkable event, if ever a life were unlikely to lead to film stardom but whose rags-to-riches story would itself make an excellent film, it would be that of Charles Bronson. He was born Charles Dennis Bunchinsky (the family would later drop the first *N*, pronouncing the name Boo-SHIN-sky) on November 3, 1921, in the coal-mining town of Ehrenfeld, Pennsylvania, better known as "Scooptown" to its inhabitants. The young Charlie was one of fifteen children born to a Lithuanian-American mother and a Russian-born father. Life was tough in Scooptown with a father who died of black lung when Charlie was only ten. As bad as it was, Charlie still embellished their existence, stating in interviews that he was practically an infant when he worked in the coal mine, when in truth he was sixteen. He also said that he had to wear his sister's hand-me-down dress to school, which also proved to be an exaggeration. He would alternately state that the love he received from his mother was what kept him going, or, depending on the mood he was in, he would say, "There was no love in my home. I was one of fifteen children, and the only physical contact I had with my mother was when she took me between her knees to pull the lice out of my hair."

Once he graduated high school, he joined the Army Air Forces, first as a truck driver and then later as a tail gunner on a B-29. He would claim to have personally shot down undocumented numbers of kamikaze pilots and to have received a Purple Heart for wounds he sustained—both unlikely, as battle flights had ended by the time he transferred to the B-29 and only reconnaissance was done. The embellishment, according to frequent costar Lee Marvin, was part of the rarely seen charm that lay beneath Bronson's well-chiseled exterior. "There's a little gleam," Marvin once said, "way back behind the eyes."

After the war, Buchinsky was only certain that he didn't want to return to Scooptown. He had an innate artistic gift that he'd expressed since childhood by sketching on anything and everything around him. He decided to study art on the GI Bill, and just as suddenly switched to drama when he happened to see a play one night. "Acting is the easiest thing I've done," he once explained. "I guess that's why I stuck with it." He shared a room with Jack Klugman while the two fledgling actors worked on Atlantic City's boardwalk. Through the late 1940s, he continued his acting classes in spite of being constantly derided for his voice and speech patterns. More insightful teachers encouraged him, taking note of his presence, his impressive physique, and that little gleam way back behind his eyes.

While taking odd jobs and acting classes in Philadelphia, he met fellow student Harriet Tendler, and in short order they courted, married, and traveled to California, where Harriet agreed to put her ambitions on hold as the young couple conspired to make Charlie a star. He continued his studies at the Pasadena Playhouse, where a teacher saw the young man's promise and got him an audition for the Gary Cooper navy comedy *You're in the Navy Now*. It was an inauspicious debut alongside Lee Marvin, but it got him more work playing thugs, Native Americans, soldiers, and various nefarious musclemen. A new agent decided that, in the midst of the Cold War, Charlie's birth name was holding him back and persuaded his client to change his name to Bronson in 1954.

Further work in film and television followed, including two short-lived series and an Emmy nomination. He also welcomed a daughter, Suzanne, and a son, Tony. Bronson painted to relieve his restlessness at seeing contemporaries gain greater status. By the early 1960s, his frustration grew in spite of a series of meaty yet still supporting roles in such testosterone-driven projects as *The Magnificent Seven* (1960) and *The Great Escape* (1963).

Bronson and Harriet divorced in 1965 and he soon took up with Jill Ireland, the blond actress wife of his friend and *Great Escape* costar, David McCallum. Ironically, the British-born Ireland was in Hollywood shooting a short-lived TV series when Bronson agreed to fly to England for the filming of *The Dirty Dozen*. Adding to his strife was the fact that his mother died just prior to filming.

He had been able to be in the Pennsylvania hospital at Mary Buchinsky's bedside for a few days as she lay dying at the age of seventy-eight. He made the arrangements and paid for her funeral, but on the day of the event, he was on a jet hurtling back to the *Dirty Dozen* set.

Asked about meeting Bronson, producer Ken Hyman recalled, "Aldrich had a trailer on the Fox lot. I worked with him in his trailer—you know, dialogue, review the script—and there's a knock on the door of his trailer. I was closest to the door, so I opened it. There was Charlie, who was his usual self, looking like he wanted to kill somebody. I said, 'Charles Bronson.' He said, 'Yeah. Who are you?' I said, 'Hopefully, I'll be your producer. My name is Ken Hyman.' He said, 'I'm here to see Robert Aldrich.' He was full of his usual charm. So I said, 'He's inside. C'mon in.' And he, without changing the expression on his face, got into the trailer, and that was that. He was not Mr. Charm. But I found it amusing. You know, that's Charlie Bronson. We became very close friends, incidentally."

The only positive thing that happened for Bronson while he was in London in 1966 was a showing of his artwork at a gallery in Beverly Hills. He was elated to discover that every painting had sold, some for as much as $3,000. One was even purchased by French actor and future Bronson costar Alain Delon. Over time, however, Bronson began to regret the sale of the paintings that meant so much to him, and he spent years buying them all back.

With *The Dirty Dozen*'s two leads secured, location filming was set to commence in April of 1966. The remainder of the cast would make up one of the most recognized, high-powered all-star casts of all time. As Hyman liked to say, "It was an interesting and tenuous time."

7

"I WAS DEALING WITH A CAST OF LUNATICS"

The rest of the cast of *The Dirty Dozen* were finalized and announced on April 4, 1966, with many of them signing on for different reasons. In the case of lead actor Lee Marvin, his reason went back to his time in the Marines. According to his son, Christopher, his father agreed to the films he made for one reason: "World War II. I could tell that World War II kind of killed his soul, being wounded and seeing his buddies dying. That's a tough one right there. I think that's why he did those films, as well as doing that for his friends and his friends that got killed."

For second lead Charles Bronson, the reason for signing on had nothing to do with the script but more to do with financial gain and the actors in the ensemble. He rarely gave interviews, but according to a close family friend, Suzie Dotan, "I know he liked *The Dirty Dozen* and *The Great Escape*. . . . He would only talk about a movie when asked. I asked him about *Dirty Dozen*. He liked working on it. . . . He just didn't know from reading the script if it would be good. He also only chose the parts based on knowing if he'd be good in the role. He also liked *The Great Escape* for the same reasons." Not coincidentally, his characters in both of these WWII–themed films had a coal-mining past.

Dotan is also quick to point out Bronson's insecurities, adding, "He just basically picked roles that he knew he could play, and wanted to play. When he got the script for *The Dirty Dozen*, he wasn't sure about it. . . . He was surprised that the movie did as well as it did and that he got the acclaim that he got, because he felt there were more famous and better actors than him cast alongside him."

One of those actors was John Cassavetes, whose reasons for agreeing to make the film were very different. "John Cassavetes was a marvelous actor," mused Ken Hyman. "He was a good writer, good director. He was also a pain in the ass." Hyman knew of what he spoke, based on the effort it took to get the maverick to agree to be in the film, but at the end of the day, Cassavetes had no choice.

Born December 9, 1929, in New York City, Cassavetes moved with his parents and older brother to their native Greece until he was seven years old, and then moved back to grow up in Port Washington on Long Island. After dabbling in sports, the dark, brooding young man took a liking to acting. When he enrolled in the American Academy of Dramatic Arts (AADA), the registering clerk told him he would have to change his name to something future casting directors would find easier to pronounce, but Cassavetes boldly replied, "They'll learn it." Such an attitude impressed fellow classmate Gena Rowlands, a formidable talent in her own right whom Cassavetes courted and eventually married in 1954. The couple remained together and often worked side by side until his death from cirrhosis of the liver in 1989.

He graduated from the AADA in 1950, the same year the Korean War started. Cassavetes had heard about a special services unit that was composed of actors and musicians, so he and his friend Harry Mastrogeorge signed up for the 306th Special Services Unit in the fall to avoid being sent to Korea. They were informed they would be trained with the infantry and could still be called into active duty within six months.

Luckily, the call never came, and the two young men helped put on shows for the stateside troops. "We reported once a week right opposite the Algonquin Hotel," recalled Mastrogeorge. "In fact we'd go in there and have a drink, and in the summertime we would go to training," he added. "John didn't like the military much. He looked just like he did in *The Dirty Dozen*, with his hair shaved right back."

The struggling young actor began to make a name for himself in early television and low-budget films. He and his friend Burt Lane even started their own nontraditional acting school, which would eventually spawn Cassavetes's first independent film. His first major lead role was in Martin Ritt's gritty urban labor drama *Edge of the City* (1957), which costarred Sidney Poitier. His reputation grew to the point that from 1959 to 1960 he starred on NBC's *Johnny Staccato* as jazz pianist Johnny Staccato, who moonlights as a private detective. He also directed several of the episodes.

His acting work enabled him to finance his first film. Over the course of two years, from 1957 to 1959, he wrote, directed, and edited *Shadows*. The groundbreaking film burnished his growing reputation and resulted in his directing such Hollywood films as *Too Late Blues* (1961) and *A Child Is Waiting* (1963). It was the latter film that inadvertently led to *The Dirty Dozen*, but not in the way Cassavetes had intended.

"He wasn't crazy about the experience, probably because

of me, as we had difficulties," legendary producer Stanley Kramer recalled in 1994. The film starred Burt Lancaster and Judy Garland as staff members at a school for developmentally challenged children. Kramer was known for well-made films dealing with controversial and socially conscious issues such as this one, and he and Cassavetes clashed often. From Kramer's perspective, "One guy has to be the driving force; that's the way I always thought to be true, anyhow. Cassavetes was young, unregimented, not accustomed to listening, and I was in his ear a lot."

Their disagreements resulted in a nasty scene when the film was screened upon its completion. An angry Cassavetes physically threatened Kramer after watching the heavily edited film and wanted his name taken off it. "I knew that would cost me," he later admitted. "In Hollywood, you don't go around publicly bad-mouthing colleagues, especially big producers like Stanley Kramer. It cost me two years of work. After the noise I made, I couldn't get a job at *Looney Tunes*. I didn't make a film for six years before getting the role in *The Dirty Dozen*."

There was actually a little more to it than that. Cassavetes did occasionally still get work on TV, and his wife was very much in demand at the time. The problem was that they had three hungry children to feed, and Cassavetes's next independent film needed money for editing, sound mixing, and other postproduction work. On top of all that, he was facing legal action from Universal Studios, to whom he owed money. They were willing to loan him out to MGM to settle the debt. "John didn't want to do a war film," said his friend and colleague Al Ruban. "They threatened to take him to court, so he did it. It worked out because of Aldrich: a super, super tough guy, but a straight shooter."

Ken Hyman was the one who had to convince Cassavetes.

"Cassavetes didn't want to do the movie. He wanted to direct a movie. I almost had a fistfight with him to get him to do it. I'd said, 'Johnny, for god's sake, this is a wonderful role. Do the movie! Put the money in your pocket, then make your movie.' And he almost didn't do it."

As for Hyman's other comment about Cassavetes being a "pain in the ass" once he was cast, Hyman said, "I said it with affection. He was a pain in the ass but he also did it with humor, if you will. He didn't like the apartment that had been found for him, so I said, 'So stay in a hotel, Johnny, but you pay for it.' He said, 'No, no, no!' I said, 'So, shut up and make the movie. C'mon, let's go.' It was happy banter back and forth."

The movie Hyman was referring to was not *The Dirty Dozen*. Luckily, Cassavetes gave in to Hyman, and the other film he was working on, *Faces* (1968), was edited at night in England while he filmed *The Dirty Dozen* during the day. The pain in the ass had turned the negative of a film he didn't want to star in into a positive. Starring in one film and using the money earned from that to create another became a Cassavetes hallmark. Doing so allowed him to become the so-called father of American independent film.

Jim Brown, the football legend cast as Robert Jefferson in the film, also had great affection for Cassavetes, but for his own reasons. "In his heart, John *was* a teacher," Brown wrote in his autobiography. "What a bold little man. Each day on the set, it was Cassavetes who set the emotional tone. He was a method actor; whatever mood his scenes called for, he would remain in that mood all day. If it was John's day to be a lunatic, he'd show up crazy, make the rest of us crazy. If he was withdrawn, we'd pull inside with him. John was our spiritual teacher. I guess he was for a lot of people who knew him."

Cast in the film that Sidney Poitier had passed on, Brown

was not nearly as method actorish as Cassavetes. Many professional athletes had attempted stardom in films, but with very little or no success. Few ever reached Brown's level of accomplishment. Not a shy man, Brown understood the reason for his film success in contrast to Poitier's. In Spike Lee's documentary *Jim Brown: All-American* (2002), Brown boldly said, "Poitier broke a lot of taboos. He had arrived, but he was not an action star. He was not a superhero. Not a loner. He was kind of a nice guy. I wanted to do all the things that we'd never done before in films." *The Dirty Dozen* put him on the path to doing just that.

Brown was born in 1936 on St. Simons Island in Georgia but moved to Manhasset, New York, with his working mother after his father abandoned them when he was eight. Playing both lacrosse and football at Syracuse University, the six-foot-two, 232-pound fullback came to national prominence in the 1957 Cotton Bowl. He went on to play nine seasons in the NFL with the Cleveland Browns and broke every rushing record there was. To many sports fans, he remains the greatest player the game has ever seen.

Brown was in Los Angeles for the Pro Bowl game in 1964 when he was approached by an executive from 20th Century-Fox. When the executive asked him if he'd like to be in the movies, the MVP fullback said he'd never acted before. The executive set Brown up with a screen test, and he was cast in a supporting role in the revenge western *Rio Conchos* (1964). The film's director, Gordon Douglas, suggested Brown get an agent, and he was recommended to the legendary Phil Gersh. When Gersh suggested his client to Robert Aldrich, Aldrich asked what else he could do besides play football. Gersh responded, "He can run faster than any of those actors."

Jim Brown was cast as the renamed character Robert T. Jefferson, and, having read and enjoyed the novel, had nothing but praise for the experience: "I loved my part. I was one of the Dozen, a quiet leader and my own man at a time when Hollywood wasn't giving those roles to Blacks. *The Dirty Dozen* is an American classic, the most popular film I've ever done, and I've never had more fun making a movie. The male cast was incredible. I worked with some of the strongest, craziest guys in the business."

The location filming also pleased Brown a great deal. He recalled, "And London was popping, every day, all night, before New York and California dove into the Revolution. The Beatles and the Rolling Stones were running all over the city, and Muhammad Ali was coming up, working out in the park, chasing girls by night. Everywhere you looked you saw miniskirts. English girls—in London they called girls 'birds'—started wearing very short skirts, all the way up their butts."

Rivaling Jim Brown in size and stature was popular TV actor Clint Walker. At six feet six inches tall and boasting a forty-eight-inch chest, Walker had the physical traits needed to play the imposing Native American Samson Posey. Walker's popular TV series *Cheyenne* (1955–62) launched the western craze of the 1950s and made him a household name. Born in 1927 in Hartford, Illinois, Norman Eugene Walker suffered through the Great Depression with his parents and twin sister, Lucy. He dropped out of high school at seventeen and joined the Merchant Marine toward the end of WWII.

After the war he traveled across the country picking up work wherever he could, including a stint as a private detective on the Long Beach, California, waterfront. While working as a bouncer at the Sands Hotel in Las Vegas, Walker met Hollywood agent Henry Willson, who offered to represent him in Hollywood.

"I got to thinking about it a couple of weeks later," Walker remembered. "I thought, I can carry a gun and a badge, where's it going to get me? Maybe shot. The guns they shoot in movies shoot blanks. Now and then you get to kiss a pretty girl. So, I quit my job and moved back to Hollywood." Within a few years he'd become the popular roaming TV cowboy Cheyenne Bodie, kissing pretty girls and shooting fake bullets. When the show ended, Walker's good looks and imposing physique got him feature film work. When offered the role of Posey, he could not have been more pleased. The script he read included a rain dance, and he very much looked forward to performing it. Ken Hyman primarily remembered that Walker not only liked to work out to maintain his physique, "He liked to snorkel and look for gold. He was a lovely guy, Clint."

The difficult role of Archer Maggott, publicly criticized and refused by Jack Palance, went to veteran character actor Telly Savalas. The proud Greek-American was born Aristotelis Savalas on January 21, 1922, on Long Island. He had been, like many journeyman actors, pursuing several different occupations following a harrowing stint in the army during WWII, an experience he refused to discuss with anyone. He eventually worked his way through the morass of villainous character roles in film and television to secure a supporting role opposite his good friend Burt Lancaster in *Birdman of Alcatraz* (1962), which earned him an Oscar nomination. The balding actor refused to wear a toupee, and by the time he played Pontius Pilate in George Stevens's *The Greatest Story Ever Told* (1965), his totally bald pate had become both permanent and iconic. It was a look he made work for him when it came to playing the demented Archer Maggott.

Completing the major roles within the dozen was popular singer Trini López, cast as Jiminez to cash in on his musical success, a practice very popular in 1950s and 1960s films. "My agent

at that time, he didn't want me to do the film," recalled Lopez.
"I said why, and he said, 'You never really done any acting, and
I think you're going to get lost in the shuffle with all those big
stars.' I said, 'Well the old saying is, if you wanna learn how to
swim, you gotta jump in the pool.' So, that's exactly what I did."

The antagonistic officers in the film were portrayed by two
veteran actors who had also seen action in WWII. Robert
Webber, cast as General Denton, had served in the Marines
and saw action on Guam and Okinawa before launching a
successful stage, film, and television acting career. Colonel Breed, the arch nemesis of John Reisman, was played by
the well-known actor Robert Ryan, who had been a Marine
drill instructor during the war. A major star in the 1940s and
1950s, Ryan was offered lesser roles in films throughout the
1960s mainly for the value his name brought to the marquee.
According to his biographer, J. R. Jones, "In western and war
movies of the late 1960s, Ryan increasingly would figure as
the odd man out, the outsider among outsiders."

Ryan's son Cheyney, the second of his three children,
recalled that his father basically did the film for the money,
which he and biographer Jones agree was in the neighborhood of $125,000. "I don't think he thought much of his role,"
Cheyney Ryan said. "The only other remark he made at the
time was that he didn't understand why the guy was a colonel,
because my father had been in the military and I think he felt,
as I did, actually, that the officer would have had a higher rank
than that."

Some cast members had worked for Aldrich a few times
before, but Richard Jaeckel, playing Reisman's majordomo,
Sgt. Clyde Bowren, was an Aldrich workhorse. Born October
10, 1926, in Long Beach, New York, Jaeckel grew up in afflu-
ence, attending mostly private schools. His family moved to

California in 1934, where he graduated from Hollywood High School. The story goes that the stocky, baby-faced blond teen-ager was working in a mail room when a casting director suggested he should screen test for a new film. Jaeckel agreed, on the condition that he return to the mail room after the test. He wound up with a role in *Guadalcanal Diary* (1943) and a career in film and television that lasted fifty years.

Rounding out the remaining roles were Robert Aldrich stalwart Ernest Borgnine as General Worden, Ralph Meeker as Captain Stuart Kinder, and George Kennedy as Major Max Armbruster. According to Kennedy, "I was involved with the *Dozen* because I had worked for Robert Aldrich. He was a friend who gave me a shot when I was first starting out, which was very meaningful for me. Originally I wanted to do the part that Telly Savalas did, the crazy nut, and Aldrich said, 'George, believe me, you could play the Savalas part, but Savalas couldn't do what I need you to do.' So, it was a very nice compliment. I would have worked for him anyway."

Like many of the cast members, Kennedy had served in WWII and saw action at the Battle of the Bulge, which he referred to as "Cattle of the Bulge." In his memoir he wrote, "We had no warm clothes: field jackets only, a wool cap under the helmet, and that was that. Nothing was flying because visibility [was] measured in arm lengths. The wind was fit for Cape Horn, the ground resisting like the impenetrable disc in *2001*. We had passwords to get around even in our own area. Sleep came borne out of total exhaustion, and the mattresses of small sticks served for two [or] three soldiers bundling. We ate K rations from a Cracker Jack–size-box—cheese and a chocolate bar. Once only, a good genie saw to it that we got C rations—canned hash, franks and beans, or stew—and cigarettes. They were in little packs of four, free. The heart-wrenching joke from a terminally wounded buddy as he was littered to a field hospital was 'Those things'll kill ya, guys.'

"Davie Reed was my best friend. The infantry encouraged you to have a buddy, to look out for each other. In the chaos, a corporal found me along the line and said, 'Reed just took a direct hit from a mortar round while bringing in chow.' I can't think of how much I still feel the pain. Over his shoulder, as he left, he added, 'The company commander wants you to write and tell his folks.'"

With the high-powered, almost entirely male cast in place, a workable script, a generous budget from MGM, and shooting set to start in England, Hyman, Aldrich, and company were ready to go. "I was dealing with a cast of lunatics," recalled Hyman with a laugh. "Every day there was a crisis that was a winner. Look at the cast. Look at Aldrich. Look at the pressures that existed."

Ultimately, as far as Hyman was concerned, the eclectic and diverse mix of personalities proved to be an advantage. "People met each other who under normal conditions would never [have] done so," remarked the producer. "Actors from New York, like Cassavetes, he probably never would have met the people from Los Angeles [unless] he happened to work with them. There was an exchange of ideas and attitudes. It was good. It was a healthy combination of people." To one observer, those exchanges included riotous arguments between Savalas and Cassavetes as to where you could get the best Greek food in New York.

There was one other aspect left to consider as Aldrich prepared to leave for England. According to dialogue director Peter Katz: "Ken Hyman said, 'I think we got a little problem.' I said, 'What is it?' He said, 'Bob Aldrich is going to show up next week and he doesn't have any actors to see for the second half of the dozen.' I made a bunch of calls. I put together a list of people for Aldrich to see, and it wasn't a big list. That pleased Bob, because we found the people that he needed very quickly."

In Ken Hyman's opinion, "The fresh faces were fillers, if you will. They had to be competent, obviously. They had to be interesting-looking. Some of them went on to build exciting careers." Indeed they did, as one of the so-called Bottom Six created a most memorable performance out of what was practically a nothing role.

One of the few female cast members, seen late in the film, had a backstory worthy of its own film. Surprisingly, she also bonded with star Lee Marvin and became a lifelong friend. Most impressive of all, the actor chosen to portray Corporal Morgan would be disappointed with the way his role was diminished from what it was in the book. However, he proved to be extremely important in a completely different, off-screen capacity.

8

THE BOTTOM SIX PLUS ONE

Robert Aldrich wrote an article for the *Los Angeles Times* just a few months before production began on *The Dirty Dozen*. Entitled "Director's Formula for a Happy Cast," he wrote about what was involved in preproduction for cast and crew and how the director makes a creative and relaxed environment possible. "First we have at least a two-week rehearsal on soundstage without interruption," he wrote. "Sitting around a long table, I impart to them my idea of the story, the characters, and the problems we face. They, in turn, contribute their ideas. Each actor has been given a script in a luxurious leather-bound cover with his or her name in gold letters on the front." True to his word, that is exactly what transpired when the cast of *The Dirty Dozen* was decided upon.

Aldrich, having worked with everyone from Burt Lancaster to Joan Crawford, had a well-established reputation in the industry. Basically, he took pride in being tough but fair. The late Eddie Albert worked with Aldrich numerous times and recalled an instance when the director's tougher side was forced to show itself. During the making of the earlier WWII–themed all-male ensemble picture *Attack!*, "We had rehearsed for a week. I think it was a Monday, and we were all there. This kid from New York, I forgot his name, was about fifteen to twenty minutes late. Aldrich didn't say anything. Tuesday he came in twenty minutes late again. Aldrich said, 'I want to have a conference. Now, this is very difficult. We have problems. We all have got to work together.' He went on very beautifully for a while and then stopped. He pointed to the actor and yelled, 'Now, you cocksuckers that come in late, I am going to kick the shit right out of you! I'll run your ass right out of this town!' I had never heard him explode like that. The kid was never late again." Such was the man who was about to deal with the diverse cast of *The Dirty Dozen*.

The remaining cast members were interviewed and hired in England and were just as distinct as the leading players. Actor Donald Borisenko had been hired to play Milo Vladek. Dubbed "the Canadian James Dean," he had been a rising star in his native land, with lucrative roles in *During One Night* (1960) and *Nine Hours to Rama* (1963). When he arrived in England for *The Dirty Dozen*, he saw the size of his role and reportedly walked off the set. He spent the next several years working variously in film and television, moving to Los Angeles in the 1970s and changing his name to Jonas Wolfe. He would later open a music club that gave Van Halen its first paying gig. He retired from acting to paint, sculpt, and write poetry, dying in 2014 at the age of seventy-four.

Replacing Borisenko as Vladek was fellow Canadian Tom Busby. He had been acting since childhood on Canada's version of *Howdy Doody*, growing into summer stock roles from the age of fourteen. His ability to affect an American accent got him roles in films such as *The War Lover* (1962) opposite Steve

McQueen, whom Busby despised. The following year he had a role in Carl Foreman's all-star WWII drama *The Victors*, boasting a young cast of such future stars as Peter Fonda, George Peppard, Albert Finney, and George Hamilton. He was next seen in *The Dirty Dozen*.

To play Glenn Gilpin, light-skinned African American actor Benito Frederico Carruthers Jr.—better known as Ben Carruthers—was chosen. Carruthers had had a leading role in John Cassavetes's *Shadows*, but Cassavetes had no input in Carruthers's being hired as one of the dozen. They simply had the same agent. He had married his *Shadows* costar Lelia Goldoni, but they divorced soon after. His second wife, Argus Spear Juillard, with whom he had two sons, also divorced him. Carruthers's sone Caine, a former musician and now a professional dog trainer, related that his father had true Spanish blood in his ancestry, accounting for the light skin and straight hair that allowed him to play Greeks, Italians, and Native Americans.

Ben Carruthers's father had worked for the OSS during the war, as he spoke seven languages. He would later become a professor at Howard University and work for the UN, hotly debating Dag Hammarskjöld. Ben Carruthers Sr. was greatly disappointed when his son dropped out of college to try to make a life in theater and music. In that pursuit, Ben Carruthers made several films, hung out in swinging London with Keith Richards and Brian Jones, and cowrote songs with Bob Dylan, all around the time in which he was cast in *The Dirty Dozen*. When Caine tells people his father was in the film, they take one look at him and cannot help but ask, "Your father is Jim Brown?"

Ben Carruthers's character would eventually get a boost due to an unforeseen circumstance while filming. It was also during filming that Carruthers had a disagreement with Charles Bronson that became so heated Clint Walker had to step in. However, when it came to Lee Marvin, he had a different opinion. Caine (nicknamed Candyman) recalls his father telling him, "Candyman, you either are rock and roll or you are not rock and roll. Lee Marvin was rock and roll."

In the role of the quarrelsome Tassos Bravos—devised to replace the novel's religious zealot, Calvin Ezra Smith—was diminutive American actor Al Mancini. An Ohio native, Mancini was in the UK writing and appearing on the popular satirical comedy show *That Was the Week That Was* due to his training in improvisational theater. When an actor was needed to add some comic touches in certain scenes of *The Dirty Dozen*, Mancini fit the bill.

Future film director Stuart Cooper recalled meeting with Robert Aldrich. Up for the role of Roscoe Lever, Cooper remembered, "I think the interview lasted probably ten minutes." Born in Hoboken, New Jersey, in 1942, he had trained at the Royal Academy of Dramatic Arts in England. Having appeared in the Michael Winner film *I'll Never Forget What's'isname* (1967) just prior to being cast in *The Dirty Dozen*, Cooper recalled, "I remember vividly in my mind there was a poster of *Baby Jane* on the wall. I had seen those pictures, so I had a little bit of a take. Keep in mind, too, that I was just out of drama school, maybe twenty. I was just, as it were, getting my feet wet. . . . I knew exactly who Bob Aldrich was, though. I didn't have a picture of him until I met him in his office. He was an absolutely warm, heavyset man, Big Bob. His trademark, which I always remembered, was that he always wore a tie to work, always."

Cooper had aspirations to direct as well as act, and would fulfill those aspirations thanks in no small part to Robert Aldrich. "Bob Aldrich had a huge impact on me as a young actor and a potential director. I probably learned more watching Bob. People ask me about directing: 'Where did you go to school?' I did it on *The Dirty Dozen*," Cooper proudly proclaimed.

Having appeared in Stanley Kubrick's *Lolita* (1962) and the Cold War thriller *The Bedford Incident* (1965), England's own Colin Maitland recalled recently, "I, like most actors, kept my ear to the ground to find out what films were coming up and if there might be any parts I could apply for, so when I read in *Variety* that *Dirty Dozen* was to be made in the UK, I immediately rang my agent and asked him to chase it up." Three weeks later Maitland's agent arranged an interview to audition for the part of Seth Sawyer, and as Maitland remembered, "Off I went to the production office to meet the various executives and director Robert Aldrich. I was never particularly nervous at interviews and auditions, and this was the same. I found out later they'd run videos of some of my work at the BBC and they were impressed."

Unfortunately, tragedy struck a few months before Maitland began work on *The Dirty Dozen*. He was working on a show for the BBC at Ealing Studios, and "I had a very serious accident," he confessed. "Falling through a glass roof and coming down about forty feet, hitting a generator on the way. Ouch!" He had fractured his skull, left eye socket, cheek, left elbow, both wrists, four ribs, and right femur. "From being a super fit young man, I left the hospital still young but with a damaged left eye and permanently bent left arm." The resulting injuries took their toll on the young thespian. "Those physical things heal, of course, and I was still fit," recalled Maitland, "but the mental trauma of the accident took much longer, and I was a long way below par while filming *Dirty Dozen*. The cheeky personality was missing and, unlike previously, I found dealing with big personalities difficult and intimidating. There were some good times, but overall I was a pale shadow of my former self."

Nevertheless, the experience was something Maitland took pride in, as his acting career didn't last much longer and he chose instead to become a successful sports reporter for the BBC. "I never really was much of an actor," he confessed. "Didn't have the kind of looks that could take you to stardom, so I doubt *Dirty Dozen* would have led me to Hollywood as it did for Donald Sutherland. He could *act!*" Maitland's assessment of his costar among the bottom six proved to be quite accurate.

"I was hired as a member of the bottom six," eighty-seven-year-old Donald Sutherland recently recalled. "I and the other five had accents that could pass for American. We all had something to say. My line was, 'Number Two, Sir!'" Sutherland would go on to have the most impressive career of all the bottom six, and he's still quite active to this day.

Born and raised in Canada, Sutherland graduated from college with a double major in drama and engineering, choosing the life of an actor. He left Canada in 1957 and spent the next decade in England, appearing opposite Christopher Lee in several low-budget Hammer horror films. Other film and TV roles followed, and when the six-foot-four Sutherland appeared on an episode of *The Saint*, he asked star and episode director Roger Moore for a favor. "He asked me if he could show it to some producers, as he was up for an important part," recalled Moore. "In fact, we were still in the middle of editing it, so I couldn't send a copy to America, as he had hoped, but they came to view a rough cut at the studio, and he got *The Dirty Dozen*."

Sutherland took full advantage of being cast as Vernon Pinkley. Neither the original novel nor the screenplay gave much background or nuance to his character, so Sutherland allowed his creative imagination to take full flower. Asked how he prepared for the practically nonexistent role, he said, "Thought. Imagined. Rehearsed. Improvised. Put him in my head and heart and soul. So he was in my head, on that screen just inside my forehead. He did all sorts of things. Like him standing guard at the French château? He'd done that on the screen in my head days before shooting, so that when we came to shoot, it was no longer me. It was him. That sounds like *crotte de boeuf*, but it's true, that's what it felt like. It felt like that in my life so far."

A further example of Sutherland's ingenuity concerned the backstory he gave the character. Asked what he thought Pinkley had been convicted for, since there's no mention of it anywhere, he said, "Stole food. It wasn't a capital crime, but he'd done it so often they wanted to get rid of him." His total understanding of what was required of him within the limited framework of what he had to work with proved the old adage that there are no small parts, only small players to be entirely true.

Costar Jim Brown had mixed feelings about Sutherland. He wrote in his memoir, "Donald Sutherland was just getting started. Aldrich was such a skilled director, he recognized Donald's acting ability and his quick wit, and encouraged him to improvise. Donald's importance added so much humor to the film [that] Aldrich repeatedly increased his part. I always considered Donald one of the finest actors I knew, but he was a distant man, difficult to know, and I don't think he's ever been truly happy."

Occasionally, even small players are more important than the roles they're required to play. A case in point is Bob Phillips. "There were things that needed to be done, so we hired him to play an MP," Ken Hyman remarked. "He took care of Lee. Lee would go out carousing, and Bob Phillips would go with him, like a bodyguard." Chicago native Phillips had his work cut out for him when it came to his friend Lee Marvin, but he was more than up to the task.

Born April 10, 1925, Phillips had been a self-defense and swimming instructor in the Marines. Unlike Lee Marvin, however, he hated his time in the Corps. Following his stint in the service, he played in the NFL for the Washington Redskins and the Chicago Bears. Phillips passed away in 2018 at the age of ninety-three but sat down for an exclusive interview with the author in 1995. He recalled in lengthy detail his time with Lee Marvin and others on *The Dirty Dozen*. "I may be a seventy-year-old fuck," he jokingly said at the time, "but I'm not senile."

In discussing his background, Phillips succinctly stated: "The story goes like this. I'm retired from LAPD. I was a detective sergeant in Pomona. Worked Sheriff's Narcotics. I was Illinois State Police. I was Adlai Stevenson's personal bodyguard. Came out here. Worked in organized crime. Intelligence. I worked undercover. The television series *Tightrope!* was based on my life." When Phillips was working undercover, one of his main informants was LA mobster and Mickey Cohen bodyguard Johnny Stompanato, who was later murdered by Lana Turner's daughter, Cheryl Crane.

While working out at his local gym, Phillips was approached by a producer about getting into acting. He suggested acting lessons for the retired cop, which he eventually took, and began getting small yet important roles on both TV and film. "We met on *The Killers*," Phillips recalled of Lee Marvin. "We were shooting that the week Kennedy got killed." He encountered Marvin again on *Cat Ballou* (1965) while continuing to get roles as henchmen and bad guys on the likes of *Batman* and the pilot for *Star Trek*.

By the time he was cast as Corporal Morgan, "I knew where

I was going," recalled Phillips. "When I left the United States [for England], I had the best part in the show. I had Morgan. Now all of a sudden they put Jaeckel in, they put Bowren in there. Originally, I was supposed to play Wladislaw. Bronson got it. Now they move me someplace else. I forgot what it was, one of the lesser dozen, Lever or Gilpin." The chess moves of casting and scene development continued for Phillips: "They moved me into the part of Morgan and cut it way down, but they used me in almost every shot. Then [Aldrich] used my voice for voice overs in scenes I wasn't even in."

Lee Marvin arrived in England earlier than the rest of the cast. According to Phillips, "Lee went over by himself. He was the only one on *The Dirty Dozen*; he went over ahead of time. The rest of us all flew over later. In my memory of it, Lee went over there first. He went over ten days, two weeks ahead of time." Marvin came early knowing that since he had been nominated for an Oscar for *Cat Ballou*, he would have to briefly return to the States for the award ceremony, so he got in a few days of preproduction for wardrobe fittings, script conferences, and the like. Before leaving, he had told columnist Sheilah Graham that he was finalizing his divorce from Betty Marvin and that his girlfriend, Michelle Triola, was absolutely not accompanying him to England. Both circumstances would change drastically once he got overseas.

In the meantime, Aldrich had another challenge to contend with at the start of production. He wanted to use his regular crew, such as director of photography Joe Biroc. "Well, the English government wouldn't allow it," Biroc said. "American crews couldn't work in England. [Aldrich] hated it. They were very, very slow. Bob didn't work that way. He was used to doing a lot of shots in a day when they only did two or three." That was merely the beginning.

The rest of the leading cast made the flight to England individually or in small groups. Phillips flew from Chicago along with Richard Jaeckel. Jim Brown made the trip during the NFL off-season and recalled, "I flew over to London with Charles Bronson. He was the strangest mofo I had ever met. I sat right next to him, [and the] man did not say one word to me. He stared straight ahead and appeared to be brooding. I spoke to him once, but I knew not to say too much."

In England and basically alone, Lee Marvin started drinking fairly early, which frustrated his director. "Lee's a charming man, very friendly, an excellent actor, very professional," Aldrich said years later. "But he can get incredibly drunk. Not every day, thankfully, but two or three days during filming. It can get really awful. When he drinks too much, all you can do is send him home." The director had worked with Marvin before and would again, despite knowing what was involved.

Marvin's close friend for many years, the late stuntman Tony Epper, said, "You buy Lee Marvin, you better budget for a couple of weeks of this crap, because again, every picture we've ever done, that's his lifestyle. This was a necessity to Lee Marvin. Sometimes he went overboard, I'll admit it. Most of the time he didn't." As for why Marvin drank, Epper added, "Lee was in pain. He had a bad back from the war and a knee injury from motorcycling, but he never said anything about it. The greatest painkiller in the world is alcohol. Believe me, it is."

Not helping Marvin's frame of mind were his marital woes, as well as his girlfriend, who was in Hawaii for a recording session. Marvin had paid for the session, but Michelle wanted to be with him in England. Bob Phillips had the same agent as Marvin at the time, and he and Ken Hyman asked Phillips to look after Marvin. Because they were friends, Phillips took up the challenge early on. "I said to [Lee], 'I'll tell you what I'll do. I'll drink with you.' We wrapped at five o'clock every night. They would have no overtime. 'I'll drink with you from five o'clock until Sunday night. But you got to promise me you'll stay sober in between time, because you're fucking ruining yourself coming in drunk.' He mumbled, 'I know, I know.' He didn't want to hear it."

Marvin and Phillips would often discuss acting techniques and bonded over what they obviously agreed on. "I've worked with so many actors and so many directors who believe it's got to be right on the money," said Phillips. "Lee and I have talked about this. Another actor would say, 'But he didn't say "now." That's my cue.' You don't have a cue. You listen to the actor when he's talking."

It may not have been the way in which Hyman or Aldrich wanted it, but the promise was kept. Marvin and Phillips worked diligently during the week and made legendary dents in the London pubs on the weekend. Of course, the incoming presences of both Betty Marvin and Michelle Triola were bound to create a few more dents of their own.

9

OSCAR AND BLACK HELEN

Principal photography on *The Dirty Dozen* was set to start on April 25, but Aldrich had planned for a two-week rehearsal period beforehand. When the cast arrived in England from the US, they were met at the airport by producer Ken Hyman. He recalled what would become a running joke as Charles Bronson arrived. Bronson took one look at Hyman and again said, "What the hell are you doing here?" Hyman recalled, "I think the magic happened the first day I saw the cast together. I mean, walking through the rehearsals, the chemistry was very exciting. We did a lot of rehearsals. It saves a lot of time on camera."

Those rehearsals took place on a soundstage at MGM-British Studios in Borehamwood, part of the Elstree Studios complex. When the cast was all sitting around the long green felt table for the script read, Clint Walker likened it to the Knights of the Round Table. It was during rehearsals that many changes were made via suggestions from the cast members as well as Aldrich. Early on, Clint Walker said he didn't feel it was respectful of Native Americans to have his character pretend to be a general. The way Donald Sutherland remembered it was, "During rehearsals, Clint Walker suggested to Bob that it was inappropriate for him to play the scene pretending to be a general, and Mr. Aldrich looked around and said, 'You, with the big ears—you do it.' That was me. My ears are largish." A script revision was then made.

Another issue in the first few days of rehearsals concerned the length of the actors' hair. According to Donald Sutherland, "We all had regulation haircuts. Charlie [Bronson] had a duck's tail—it was the style back then, though I thought it was more 1967 than 1943. At one of the table reads, in front of all of us, one of Mr. Aldrich's black phones rang. He picked it up. Held it to his ear. Listened, put his hand over the mouthpiece, and yelled down the table to Charlie that it was his LA lawyer on the phone, asking whether Charlie wanted him to fly over to give him a haircut, or would he prefer to get a professional from London to do it? Charlie threw his hands in the air. What could he do? Socially, the odds were stacked against him. He was a Polish coal miner's son."

It was also the beginning of award season in Hollywood for the previous year's films, which added yet more gasoline to the considerable fire of Lee Marvin's success. When Marvin was named Best Actor in a Comedy for *Cat Ballou* at the Golden Globes in February of 1966, he graciously accepted his award and quipped, "Oh—I didn't think it was all *that* funny." Other awards followed, and the goodwill and media attention he gained through columnists' write-ups proved his publicist Paul Wasserman's prediction: Marvin was nominated for an Academy Award for Best Actor. According to several sources, his salary for *Cat Ballou* had been $87,000 for the twenty-four-day shoot. Following his Golden Globe win and Oscar nomination, he was getting $350,000 for *The Dirty Dozen*.

Marvin knew that comedic performances rarely won Oscars, and his fellow nominees were some of the best actors in the industry. His competition consisted of Laurence Olivier for *Othello*, Richard Burton for *The Spy Who Came In from the Cold*, Rod Steiger for *The Pawnbroker*, and Marvin's *Ship of Fools* costar Oskar Werner. Handicapping such competition, Marvin at first said, "Two will get you twenty that I'll win no Oscar. The competition is too stiff, but I'll be there." He then predicted the winner would be Werner, graciously proclaiming, "I want to be in competition with the best. I'm in tremendous company . . . I think I have a fifty-fifty chance." Four days before the awards show, he said, "The men with whom I'm competing for the Academy Award can all act circles around me, but this is the land of milk and honey. If you have the right gimmick, you're in. I never got out of high school, and here I am making many more times the money the president of the United States makes. It's pretty ridiculous, really, but that's how it is."

On the night of the Oscars, Marvin flew in from the London location to fulfill his promise to take his wife to the awards ceremony, even though by that time they had already separated. However, just a few hours before the show, Lee informed Betty that Michelle had told him she would commit suicide if he didn't take her instead. Betty recalled with a laugh, "I just said, 'Oh, Lee, I think you should reconsider it.' I took the dress, folded it up, and put it away. I put on my sweats or something. It wasn't a big deal to me that I didn't go to the Academy Awards. It was just the whole thing he did was so tacky. A friend called, and I said to him, 'I think I'm going to dress the kids up in something shabby and I'll go in some rags. We'll go down to the Academy Awards, and I'm going to sit inside and have the kids say, "Hi, Daddy!"' My friend said, 'You wouldn't do that.' I said, 'Oh, I don't know. I probably could . . .'"

Betty graciously changed her mind, and Lee sat nervously chain-smoking and hiding the cigarette under Triola's dress during the ceremony. To ease his tension, he leaned over to fellow nominee Rod Steiger and whispered that if Steiger won, he would trip him on the way to the stage. When Julie Andrews announced the nominees for Best Actor, Marvin's agent Meyer Mishkin recalled, "Lee was on the aisle. I was next to him, and then Michelle, and then my wife. So, he's sitting on the aisle, they announce the winner is Lee Marvin. He gets up and buttons his jacket. He always had an attitude with it. He buttons his jacket, and says to me, 'I love you, you cocksucker.' I said to him, 'Go get it!'"

He came to the stage to the largest applause of the evening. Tears welled up in his eyes, and when the applause had died down, he composed himself and famously said, "Thank you, thank you all, very much. I don't want to take up too much of your time. There are too many people to correctly thank for my career. I think, though, that half of this belongs to a horse, someplace out in the Valley. Thank you." After his acceptance, he left the stage, got to a phone, and immediately called Betty to thank her for all that she had done for his career. He tried calling his father, but Robert answered and told him that though Monte had watched the acceptance, he refused to come to the phone when he saw that it was Michelle and not Betty in the audience. Backstage, Marvin fielded the usual barrage of questions from the Hollywood press corps as cameras flashed and fellow Oscar winners congratulated each other.

"He certainly didn't act like that tough, hard-drinking character of *Cat Ballou*, because he cried more backstage than Shelley Winters," wrote columnist Sheilah Graham. "I asked him if he thought the award would change his life, and he said, 'Hell, yes. I'm not Superman.'" In the limo on the way to the after-party, Meyer was able to get Monte on the phone, who told his son how proud he was of him. At a red light, Marvin then saw Rod Steiger in the car next to him, hunched over in the backseat and apparently crying. Marvin tapped the glass, and when Steiger made eye contact, he held up his Oscar and beamed.

The next morning, a slightly hungover Marvin was photographed at LAX on his way back to London's Heathrow Airport receiving the impromptu surprise of a bridal bouquet of flowers from his best friend, actor Keenan Wynn. Back in London, he rented a flat that was within a short walking distance of a nearby pub.

Marvin's publicist, the late Paul Wasserman, said in 1996, "When Lee was in London for *The Dirty Dozen* he lived near Julie Christie. Since they were both Oscar winners, they flew back on the same plane . . . if memory serves me correctly." The two Oscar winners also appeared in a documentary about swinging London entitled *Tonite Let's All Make Love in London* (1967) when Lee returned. He's interviewed in costume for *The Dirty Dozen* and is also seen in a posh British nightclub looking extremely bored.

Back at rehearsal, "We all arrived on time. Lee had already shown up," recalled Stuart Cooper. "He was sitting in his chair at the end of the table, right next to Bob's chair. The Oscar was plunked right on the green felt. He looked like he hadn't slept in days, and he'd probably had far too much to drink, and he just sat there with his Oscar. Everybody congratulated him, of course. He didn't say a word. It was just an unbelievable moment. It was so wonderfully cute and done Lee Marvin–style."

Bob Phillips grumbled to himself about how the part of

Corporal Morgan had been slimmed down during the readings. Phillips had made friends with John Cassavetes, who offered the actor some sage advice. He told Phillips he had a right to be bitter, but there was something else; as Phillips recalled, "Johnny told me, 'If you get mad, Bobby, and they ask you, "How's *The Dozen?*" tell them it's the greatest film and the biggest part . . .' They won't even know six months from now. Don't go back and bad-mouth Aldrich.' That parlayed me into a lot of good parts."

It was during the rehearsal period that Lee Marvin and Charles Bronson had their first of several run-ins. A military advisor had said the proper command for drill instruction was "Dress right!" Charles Bronson, who had been in the Army Air Forces, disagreed and said it was "Right dress!" Former Marine Lee Marvin said the advisor was correct. This debate went on for a while until Aldrich had had enough. According to Stuart Cooper, "Bob, at the precisely perfect moment, stepped right between their two faces. They're right at each other, [and he] put his face right in and his chin jutted out like a bulldog and he said, 'I don't give a fuck if it's dress right or right dress. You do it the fucking way we tell you to do it.' That was exactly what he said. Those were the words, and it was done. Everybody just kind of splintered off. These things happen, but he was just right in there."

During a break in rehearsals, Colin Maitland humorously recalled, "We went to the commissary at MGM for lunch, and chicken was on the menu. Clint Walker said, 'I'll have some chicken.' Clint, as we all know, is a huge man, six-foot-six or so—talk about being built like a barn door. The waiter came along and Clint said, 'No, I want *a* chicken. Not just *some* chicken. I want *a* chicken.' So they brought him a whole chicken, which he then ate."

The rehearsals proved most fruitful, according to Ken Hyman. He was present every day of rehearsal and filming and remembered, "It was marvelous to watch the camaraderie develop, where the cast at times behaved as though they were the Dirty Dozen." By the time principal photography began, all involved were totally prepared. Just to keep things light, Aldrich decided that the very first shot would be the scene of the dozen lined up for inspection, but set it up slightly differently. Charles Bronson liked to wear boxing shoes during run-throughs. Knowing that, Aldrich had the extremely tall Clint Walker and Donald Sutherland standing next to him. The comparatively diminutive Bronson looked right, looked left, threw his hands in the air, and stalked off muttering, "Fuck this." It took another ten minutes to set up the shot correctly, as Aldrich and the crew could not stop laughing.

Aldrich wasn't the only one prone to pranks. Bob Phillips remembered an elaborate prank he was involved in with Lee Marvin and Richard Jaeckel. "I'd come on the set, [and] these English guys would have these bull necks and brains about this big," remembered Phillips. "Lee would say, 'The goddamned son of a bitch. Can you believe it? All the fucking years Jaeckel and I have been together!' I'd say, 'What's wrong?' He'd say, 'I went out last night with him to the White Elephant and he groped me!' Then it came down to do the scene, and before action, Jaeckel gooses the British guy and says, 'It's only a rumor.' The guy can't say a word, and Jake's got him, you know?"

It was also imperative that the actors familiarize themselves with the props they had to use. One of the armorers for the film was British stuntman Jim Dowdall, who to this day corrects people who, thanks to IMDb.com, think he was Lee Marvin's stunt double: "This is complete nonsense. I was never Lee Marvin's stunt double. My first job in the film business was as an armorer, working with guns. So, I worked on *The Dirty Dozen*, which was my first film. I worked with Lee Marvin as an armorer, not as a stunt double." Having left school at the age of sixteen, Dowdall had been a lion tamer and an acrobat before entering the film industry. "I had just begun working for a movie armory company—Bapty and Co.—as an apprentice armorer, and *Dirty Dozen* was my first movie, so I was very green!"

Being so green, Dowdall learned an important lesson in the way in which various egos deal with props. Asked about how the cast handled the weapons, Dowdall recalled, "For them, they were just another prop and didn't get too flustered if anything jammed." When he introduced himself individually to each cast member to instruct them in the use of the grease guns, he cited two examples. "I had already been to Charles Bronson and Donald Sutherland. Charles Bronson was very rude: 'I know how to fire a gun, kid, so piss off.' I said, 'Okay,' and I went to Lee Marvin's room." Marvin had clearly been drinking, as a half-empty bottle of Jack Daniels sat next to him at 10:00 a.m., along with a cigar smoldering atop a prop tripod. Dowdall introduced himself and explained his purpose. The actor responded, "Okay, kid. Do your thing."

Over the next several minutes, Dowdall said, "I start telling him about this particular M-3 grease gun, and he's nodding his head, very knowledgeable, 'Mm-hmm. Yeah, I'm getting it.' I'm going, 'You gotta be very careful, as the empty casings come out the side and they can hit people in their hearts, blah, blah, blah.' Remember, he's sitting down looking up at me, and my eye line is down at him. He puts his arms out and he takes the weapon off me. And he's now talking to me, and he strips it down without looking at it. Puts all the various parts on the table, and he looks down at it and I look down at it. Then he looks up again and continues the conversation. He puts it all back together again, effectively blindfolded, and then hands it back to me. I go, 'Right [*clears throat*], let's move on,' not realizing he was in the Marine Corps during the war. He was wounded. He was decorated, and he's a gun nut. It proved to be a most interesting relationship."

As the filming progressed, those personality differences became even more pronounced. "Bronson, however, was really rude and indifferent and would throw his grease gun on the ground if it malfunctioned. We had two really reliable grease guns, and eventually we put a tiny spot of paint on the back of the magazine housing along with the magazine that always seemed to work, and for years after, they were always referred to as Marvin's and Bronson's guns, as we knew they'd always work."

Stuntman Tony Epper was most familiar with Marvin's prowess with firearms. He recalled back in 1994: "He knew weapons. If he had one, he'd be one of the few people I'd trust with one in his hand. He could field dress a .45 faster than anybody I ever knew. . . . He had moves with firearms that were worked out. I remember he had a Thompson [submachine gun] . . . He would do things, little cute things that had nothing to do with the military. You ever watch him handle a gun? Those were well-thought-out moves."

It being England, the weather did not always cooperate for Aldrich, and on more than one rained-out occasion Marvin could be found at the nearest pub. His partner in crime this time was Bob Phillips. The two ex-Marines frequented many of the local watering holes, and Phillips recalled one particular night on which disaster was barely averted. They had been drinking and winning at darts all night, angering the locals but earning the affection of the bartender, a sixty-year-old, six-foot-tall brunette-beehive-wig-wearing Lee Marvin fan whom Phillips had dubbed "Black Helen."

When a patron started removing the darts from the board while Marvin was still playing, a dart landed in the man's coat between his shoulder blades. A voice then immediately rang out, "The Yank stabbed me, mate!" The owner of the voice was taller than Marvin and huskier than Phillips and proceeded to advance on the duo. "Lee swings with a John Wayne round-house right. Lee missed him by three feet. Not that the guy ducked or anything. Lee sailed over right behind him. I went in and I hit that son of a bitch right, and he went down and out. Lee stands up and he looks down at the guy. 'Anybody else? Who's next?' Honest to god, in his best passionate style. Well, here comes about five or six of them. Boy, out of nowhere, with her beehive, is Black Helen. Nobody's going to punch out Lee. She saved our ass. I grabbed Lee and I said, 'Let's get out of here.' He said, 'What about our drinks?' He's worried about the drinks!" Thanks to Helen, they were able to beat a hasty retreat and make it back to their hotel unscathed.

Marvin and Phillips appeared on the set each day ready to work, despite nighttime adventures such as that one. Phillips also bonded with Marvin through their mutual war experiences and their schoolboy antics. "Bob Aldrich used to always say 'Zabba, zabba, zabba' about a scene," recalled Phillips. "Then he'd shoot it and say, 'That's a thing of beauty. Print it. Next shot.' We'd imitate him when he wasn't on the set. Lee and I would talk, 'Zabba, zabba.' One of those kids playing one of the Dozen would walk up and we'd say, 'We're running lines.' We'd always catch somebody with that."

They also took to playfully calling Charles Bronson "Charlie Sunshine," due to his often dour disposition. Years later, Marvin recalled about his frequent costar, "He wants to intimidate you.

We were sitting in London once in a very posh club, wearing black suits, talking to a girl. Charlie says, 'Yeah, sweetheart, it's tough lying on your side in a coal mine.' I said, 'Jesus, Charlie. You ain't been in a coal mine in thirty years. You drive around in a Rolls Royce.'"

Further proof of Marvin and Phillips's arrested development was a childish stunt they called "Bull Nelson." According to Phillips, "Lee would walk up to a guy. He'd say to me, 'Hey, Bob, here's one guy you can't get the Bull Nelson on.' We'd stake a guy out for two or three days. The guy would swell up, flexing his muscle. I'd say, 'Well, I don't know.' Lee would say, 'I betcha can't get the Bull Nelson on him.' The guy would say, 'What's the Bull Nelson?' Now we got everybody gathered around. Nobody else is in on it. So, now we got the guy set up. 'All right, I'll take over from here. You got to work around, and then you got to break the hold.' He takes his money out and everything. What I do is I get a full nelson on him. Only what I would do is take all the leverage out of your neck. I can control you but I'm not going to hurt you, and you can't hurt yourself. I'd say, 'Ready?' He'd say, 'Yeah.' The minute he'd start, I'd go like this." Phillips then proceeded to mime dry humping the unsuspecting victim like a bull does a cow. Asked about the stunt's origin, Phillips simply said, "It's old, old, old. Maybe off the streets of Chicago or something."

Lisa Ryan, daughter of actor Robert Ryan, remembers that her father would often laugh to himself and mutter, "What a character" whenever Marvin's name was mentioned. She discovered what he meant when visiting the London set one morning: "I was just standing around, and then Lee Marvin just sort of walked over to me and was sort of leaning over me. He seemed drunk, and I knew who he was. I was just sort of like, 'Oooh, Lee Marvin!' He was like, 'Oh, what are you doing here?' I mainly remember that he was kind of listing toward me. I wasn't upset or anything. I thought it was really cool that I was standing there talking to Lee Marvin. The next thing I remember is my dad came marching over and said, 'Lee! That's my daughter!' I remember he literally jumped backward. I mean it really was like he got zapped with a cattle prod or something. He just jumped backward and kind of stumbled away. That was the end of it. I don't recall anything unpleasant. I think it was funny. I think maybe my dad thought it was funny, too."

Costar Clint Walker remembers the experience of working with Marvin as a pleasant one, saying: "Lee's a pro. Sometimes there's a problem that'll pop up that you simply don't anticipate. Maybe the gate on the compound fence swings the wrong way, so you got to change a scene a little bit or something. Other than that, as I say, Lee always knew his lines. I think there were a few times he may have suggested something to Bob Aldrich. I think, for the most part, Bob went along with it. Don't forget that Lee had a military background. He was right at home with what he was doing. . . . I think everybody had a great deal of respect for Lee. Usually, what he did or said made sense. I can't even remember any problems or friction or any real difference of opinion. . . . I think everybody got along quite well."

Walker's major scene in the film involved Marvin's character taunting him to lose his temper and stab him with a knife. Walker recalls: "I had cut my finger the night before fixing a chicken for my supper. I had to go to the hospital. I think it took about five stitches in my right thumb." As Aldrich explained to Walker how the scene would work, "He grabbed my thumb instead of my hand. He started leading me around by it, and Lee starts tapping Bob on the shoulder and saying, 'Um, Bob . . .' Bob kept on going, and he said, [*louder*] 'Bob!' He said it a third time, and Bob stopped and said, 'What do you want, Lee?' Lee says, 'Let go of Clint's thumb.' Bob looked and said, 'Why?' Lee said, 'Because he cut it last night and he had five stitches taken in it.' Bob said, 'Oh!' [and] let go, and then started laughing. That was the beginning of the scene. So as you can see, Lee certainly had consideration for his fellow man." According to Clint's daughter, Valerie Walker, when the scene was finally shot, "he did say he felt like he was being tossed around by an ant."

Walker's then sixteen-year-old daughter, Valerie, had briefly joined her father for the filming. "I'd never traveled in time zones," she recalled. "I got there in the middle of the night, and my time zones were all messed up. Dad insisted on trying to be a dad and feed me. Of course, he had these health food things going on, and he made me tuna fish and sunflower seeds on some sort of salad, and pureed pineapple. I threw it up. He felt so bad, but my system was all out of whack."

She also remembered a particular adventure she had while in Europe: "Dad was offered a four-day trip to pick three countries he might want to go to during one of those quiet times. Dad had an English girlfriend there named Pauline. She was a model, I think. So instead of his going, he gave those passes to Pauline and me. I got to choose which countries I wanted to go to. Yeah, there were a lot of things Dad probably did while he was filming when I was not there. Like I said, I was there for about a week or so. I chose Paris because everybody always goes to Paris. And then I chose Berlin, because my dad was a conservative and I wanted to see the Berlin Wall in that country there. I learned a lot in Berlin because we drove up to the wall. It was still up then, and they had a platform they'd built up with binoculars that the tourists could go up and look across the wall at these burned-out buildings where the [East Germans] were going back and forth inside with their guns and soldiers [were] marching back and forth.

"I remember them telling us about how many people had been shot from the [East German] side trying to climb the wall. So, I was feeling very indignant. I'm up there glaring at this soldier walking back and forth with his rifle. I'm looking through binoculars at him, and he turns around and brings [his] binoculars up to his face, and he's looking back at me, and all of a sudden he raises his hand and waves. And I thought, 'Oh, for god's sake, he's just a poor guy that's stuck there.' These are just people. I told my dad about it, and he said we're all victims of tyrants."

Valerie's parents were in the midst of a divorce at the time, as were several other individuals involved in the film. Ben Carruthers, Charles Bronson, and others were either getting divorced, separated, or remarried. Both Ken Hyman and Robert Aldrich had recently married, with Aldrich's German-born wife, Sibylle Siegfried, writing and singing a song for the film.

However, when it came to domestic conflict, all others paled in comparison to that of Lee Marvin. In the midst of filming, both his soon-to-be ex-wife and his live-in girlfriend came to London at the same time. As in a badly written farce, each of them never encountered the other, thanks mostly to Bob Phillips.

PART III

Reception

10

"BRONSON HAS MORE LINES ON HIS FACE THAN I HAVE IN THIS PICTURE"

The number of challenges Aldrich and company dealt with while making *The Dirty Dozen* mounted daily. The aforementioned weather was one of the worst. Filming took place primarily in Hertfordshire, approximately fifteen miles north of London, and Trini López recalled, "I remember the difficulties were mainly with what they called 'the Bloody Weather of England.' We would go on location, drive way out, and we wouldn't shoot one foot of film because we couldn't see in front of our faces." A shoot that was slated to last four months ran over schedule by another four, as well as over budget. The original budget—$4 million, an impressive figure in its day—doubled to $8 million before everything was in the can.

Also an issue on the location was the anger of local residents. Driving the trucks, cars, and equipment through the quaint, sleepy villages of Hertfordshire every day resulted in ruined lawns and mud-spattered roads and homes. Hoping to win Britain's best-kept village competition, the local council of Borehamwood surveyed the area and declared it had never been such a mess. The cleanup didn't help the film's budgetary issues. When it came to such cost overruns, Ken Hyman recalled the heat that came from MGM: "To a degree, but when they saw the rushes I think they mellowed a bit." In other words, it may have been expensive, but it was determined to be worth it.

For the cast, several scenes also proved problematic. "We were told the different things we're supposed to carry, forty-pound pack and an M-1, and this and that," said Trini López. "You know, I'm a singer. I never held a rifle in my hands in my life! We all got along so well that it became like a natural thing. The only time I remember that was kind of tough was when Charles, myself, and some of the other guys . . . had to come down this big, big, long hill, and we were carrying this forty-pound pack thing on our back. I've never been in the service, by the way. So we had to run like [bats] out of hell down this hill, and I know that if I had tripped, I would've broken my neck. But Charles, man, he just went down like a rocket. He was a tough guy. He was in good shape. And so I lucked out that I never got hurt."

As an example of how unprepared he was for certain aspects of the film, Colin Maitland recalled shooting the scene in which he and López had to train in hand-to-hand combat. "I was paired with Trini López, who was doing his first film and had never been schooled in 'movie fighting.' He was told to twist my arm behind my back and use his forearm across my throat, but instead of doing it without pressure, he enthusiastically went at it, and I found myself turning blue before Aldrich yelled 'Cut!' López was very sorry afterward, and he was too nice a guy to hold a grudge against."

When the weather was uncooperative or when the actors

were between scenes, marathon poker games took place among anyone not needed on set. According to Colin Maitland, the game ran continuously from April to late September. The likes of Telly Savalas, Clint Walker, Charles Bronson, and John Cassavetes could be found sitting in at any given time. "The stakes were too rich for my blood, though," said Maitland. "I once lost three hundred pounds [roughly $1,000 at the time] in ten minutes and decided to take up chess instead. That didn't help much, as Jim Brown beat me at that!"

Maitland would have been better served to do what Donald Sutherland did. "If I remember right, I was the only one who sat in on the stuntmen's daily penny-ante poker games," Sutherland recalled. "That was probably because I was led there by my stuntman, Maurice Dunster, aka Mo. I didn't see them after the film wrapped, except [for] one. We seemed to have a good relationship, then he borrowed some money and I never saw him again, except once on the street. But when he saw me, he turned his tail and ran. Sometimes it's like that."

When he wasn't needed on set, John Cassavetes was editing his next film, *Faces*. He did occasionally join other cast members to drink and carouse in the London casinos, however. Cassavetes's friend Larry Shaw recalled, "John could outdrink anyone. A guy like Lee Marvin drank as much as John, but you could tell he was drunk. With John, you never could."

Stanley Kubrick was filming *2001: A Space Odyssey* (1968) for MGM on a nearby soundstage, and Cassavetes joked with a friend about their different styles of directing. Kubrick had turned down an elaborate set of the moon MGM had built, because he wanted a different moon. "When I want a moon," joked Cassavetes, "I go outside and shoot what's up in the sky. But Stanley's a genius, while I'm a bum from Port Washington who grew up on the Long Island railroad."

During rehearsals and filming with Aldrich and the cast, Cassavetes proved to be surprisingly enthusiastic. "Aldrich liked me a lot and made me feel free," he later said. "Working with people like Lee Marvin and Charles Bronson, Telly Savalas, you can't fail to have fun. We were all greedy: There aren't going to be that many big parts in a picture, so you all fight for some screen time. Bob used to call us 'the animals,' more like a football coach than a maestro. He'd say, 'Who wants to do this?' Everyone would just look at each other, too afraid to move, and I'd jump forward, and someone would shout some obscenity. I didn't care." He also stated, with classic Cassavetes exaggeration, "I started off with three lines and ended up with a whole lot more."

Possibly the best compliment paid to Cassavetes came from Lee Marvin. Costar Stuart Cooper recalled, "I remember Lee saying that Cassavetes was a huge help to him because of John's spontaneity and the way he'd stop and change things. He would bring stuff to Lee that Lee could work off of. It really kind of brought the conflict of the Dozen to a single voice to him."

Cooper, an aspiring director himself, felt that he was in the right place at the right time. "At that time the *Dozen* was in production, in preparation, shooting, and postproduction, because I think they did some post on the MGM lot," recalled Cooper, "Kubrick was shooting *2001* with John Alcott photographing, who became my mentor later." Other films in production at the time on MGM's London lot included *Casino Royale* and an obscure little picture, *The Fearless Vampire Killers*, by Roman Polanski and starring the late Sharon Tate.

"So, it's very interesting what other movies were being made at that particular time at the MGM studios. It was an incredible time to go to lunch in the canteen . . . and see all these people and all these great movies being made.

Great characters, quite special. You have to remember this is late-sixties London, and London was abuzz. There was a huge filmmaking community living in London at the time. 20th Century-Fox was there, Warner Bros.—there was just a lot of activity going on." Cooper would take his experiences from London and later direct the D-Day film *Overlord* (1975) in conjunction with John Alcott. It has since been heralded as one of the most innovative war films ever made.

Jim Brown passed his free time staying in shape with daily workouts. On one occasion he did so with his friend, visiting heavyweight champ Muhammad Ali. Ali was in London for a fight—the first world championship bout in England in several decades—which Ali won.

Clint Walker's daughter recalled Brown offering to play catch with her when she was visiting. "They were building a set for the stockade," Valerie Walker recalled. "While they were building that set, the actors were standing out in a field, and everybody was waiting around. Jim Brown gave me a football. I'm a sixteen-year-old girl and kind of shy, and he says, 'Okay, I'm going to go run along.' He's running backward and says, 'Throw me a pass.' I didn't know I could throw that well. I threw one and it went over his head and kept going. What I didn't know, or Jim Brown didn't know, was that they had a big roll of barbed wire back there, and Mr. Brown ran backward and sat in that. I thought he was going to kill me, but he was so nice about it."

On a more serious note, Brown was becoming the focus of intense media scrutiny. Sportswriters were speculating whether he would be able to return to the Cleveland Browns in time for training. Art Modell, who owned the team at that time, said in 2002, "[Brown] was determined to come back and play football, but they ran into difficulty, weather, and they had to delay

production. He called and said, 'I can't come back until late
September or October.' I said, 'Look, I can't make an exception.' [Browns coach] Blanton Collier and I discussed it. To
have him show up in October would be unfair to the other players who went through the two-a-day ordeal of training camp."

Jim Brown's point of view was that if the team needed him,
he would consider coming back. "Art didn't pay any attention. . . . He gave me an ultimatum. He sent Carroll Rosen-
bloom over to talk to me, who was the owner of the Colts, I
think, at that time. He came over and knew in two minutes I
wasn't coming back." Modell's solution was to suspend Brown
and fine him one hundred dollars a day for every day he missed.
"That's lunch money today," recalled Modell. "He resented that.
The next day [June 17, 1966,] he held a press conference."

At the press conference on the set of *The Dirty Dozen*, Jim
Brown made it official, stating, "My original intention was to
try to participate in the 1966 NFL season. But due to circumstances, this is impossible." Thus, Jim Brown left pro football
to embark on a film career and philanthropic work on behalf
of African Americans. As he said years later, "When I left,
I left gloriously, because it was fine. I had done nine years; I
was MVP of the league. Twenty-nine years old and we won
the championship. I'm on my own terms." Modell is on record
as saying he made a mistake. The announcement made major
headlines. It also brought the film the kind of publicity you
couldn't buy at any price.

Actually, Brown had already mentioned it in an article
entitled "'I'm Ready to Quit Football'—Jim Brown" by Maggie Hathaway published in the African American periodical the *Los Angeles Sentinel* in January, three months before
photography for *The Dirty Dozen* began. Sportswriters either
failed to notice it or simply continued to speculate on their

own in hopes of getting an exclusive. Had they been aware of the piece, they would have read this direct quote: "Mag, I am ready to quit football. The only reason I have not quit before is because of the consideration and respect I have for my owner, Art Modell." That respect clearly vanished as the shooting of *The Dirty Dozen* dragged on.

Lee Marvin knew Brown had made the right decision, and said as much when asked about it on location. His logic was that Brown had a future in film and was a natural actor. Watching games on Sundays, Marvin had noticed how Brown would react exaggeratedly after a tackle and limp back into the game. Brown later admitted that when he was tackled, he purposely moved more slowly into the huddle so the other team wouldn't know if he was really hurt.

That, of course, was not always the case. Cheyney Ryan recalled something his father had told him as he and Brown became friends during the making of the film. Before Brown had officially announced his retirement, Cheyney recalled, "I remember Dad saying explicitly that Brown said he wasn't going to go back. What he did was, he actually took off his shirt and showed Dad what his body looked like from being all beat up. I remember my dad was a boxer, so that was the kind of thing that impressed him."

As filming on *The Dirty Dozen* progressed, so too did the challenges. Running over budget and over schedule, Aldrich let his frustration be known to the producer, Ken Hyman. It was not merely the weather that irked Aldrich. British governmental rules required Aldrich to use a British director of photography; in this instance, it was Edward "Ted" Scaife. Scaife had begun his career in the sound department, but in 1940 began working in the camera department. He lent his talent as a camera operator to such innovative films as Michael

Powell and Emeric Pressburger's *Black Narcissus* (1947) and Carol Reed's postwar thriller *The Third Man* (1949). He would eventually become a full-fledged cinematographer collaborating with the likes of John Huston no less than five times. Working with American directors shooting overseas became Scaife's stock-in-trade. Aldrich was frustrated by the amount of time it took Scaife and his crew to set up scenes, but he did like the way the scenes turned out.

The issue that Aldrich wanted to bring to Hyman's attention concerned the estimated length of the finished film based on the number of scenes that were being shot. In a memo to Hyman, Aldrich wrote, "We now have a script that time-wise runs in excess of 3 hours. To me, this makes no sense at all, and it is a waste of your time, my time, and Metro's money. Consequently, I feel severe and drastic cuts should be made NOW, concerning what will reflect the cost, and of course, the shooting schedule. Therefore, I propose the elimination of the following: Everything that has to do with Lady Margot; everything that lies between the dirty dozen capturing Breed's HQ and the Last Supper; Everything at the Jump School, from the humiliation of the false inspection of the troops to the fight in the latrine. My opinion that the picture can only benefit from these cuts is certain to save the estimate of 20 minutes of film time and at a minimum, eight days' shooting."

According to Colin Maitland, the schedule and budget issues were about more than what Aldrich mentioned. "Bob Aldrich believed in doing a master, as every director does, and then he would do a take from every conceivable angle," recalled the actor. "Even if it was a simple two-person shot, he would get a crane and he would shoot directly down. He'd dig a pit and he would shoot up. And of course this added to the overall length of the movie. I'm sure it must have driven the producer crazy, but that was his way. He was a master craftsman, and it showed, I think, in the movie."

As far as producer Hyman was concerned, "I was very happy to extract any good idea that he had, and I would ignore what I didn't like. . . . Hey, listen, if you know how to get along with people, life is simple. If you want to have problems, they're easier." In the end, Lady Margot and certain events at Breed's jump school were indeed eliminated, but the fight in the latrine and the humiliating fake troop inspection remained.

The compromises agreed to by Aldrich and Hyman meant that the role of Cpl. Morgan was cut down considerably—so much so that when *Variety* columnist Army Archerd asked Phillips about it, he quipped, "Charles Bronson has more lines on his face than I have in this picture." When Bronson asked Phillips if he really said that, Phillips responded, "No, that was some publicity guy."

Lee Marvin had his own unique ability to deal with the media, as Robert Phillips illustrated with a bawdy anecdote. A female reporter from New York came to the London set to interview Marvin. According to Phillips, she continued to pepper Marvin with embarrassing questions about his marriage. Marvin leaned over to Phillips and whispered, "Watch me get her." Later that night, Phillips went to meet Marvin for dinner and was informed the actor was in his limo. When Phillips opened the car door, the reporter was on her knees performing oral sex on Marvin, who had an "I-told-you-so" smile on his face.

Phillips may have had more time on his hands because he wasn't always needed on set, but he was certainly kept busy by Lee Marvin. Earl Wilson reported in his column that Lee had arranged for his soon-to-be ex-wife to come to London for a possible reconciliation. Phillips recalled how it all played out:

"Now all of a sudden he comes to me in a panic. 'Betty's coming. What am I going to do?' He says Michelle's booked in. He had her over in Hawaii, as I remember it. She was going to come right on over, and he didn't know what to do." Triola and Marvin had many long-distance phone calls about a reunion until she persuaded Marvin to arrange for her to come to England immediately. In the midst of this dilemma, he enlisted the aid of his costar, bodyguard, and loyal friend, Bob Phillips. In essence, Phillips became a beard for his buddy's wife, escorting Mrs. Marvin all over London from a home base at the Dorchester Hotel. "It's almost too much to ask of a friend," recalled Phillips. He and Betty Marvin saw many plays together in London, courtesy of Robert Aldrich's generosity.

Miraculously, Betty Marvin and Michelle Triola did not once encounter each other, according to Bob Phillips. On occasion, Phillips would procure a date—a retired LAPD detective named Bette—to accompany Lee and Michelle to dinner. Marvin picked up the tab for the foursome at one of the hippest Italian eateries in London. The excursion also allowed Marvin to show off his epicurean skills. His menu suggestions delighted his guests, as did his knowledge of the popular wines of the day. As though he were a trained sommelier, Marvin ordered several bottles of Soave Bolla for the table. "After about the third or fourth bottle," remembered Phillips, "Lee turned to Bette and said, 'Now, remember the name. You know how, right? Just remember Suave Balls.' Oh, she told that story for years."

Not all of Phillips's recollections of being in London during the *Dirty Dozen* shoot were as pleasant. He had a run-in with Jim Brown that he retold with much bitterness. Brown had been harassing a young woman by restraining her between his massive thighs. Phillips, witnessing the scene, lost his temper and said to Brown, "If I have to get out of this chair, I'm going to kill you." Despite his size advantage, Brown let the girl go, saying to fellow ex–football player and retired undercover cop Phillips, "I believe you."

Then there was Ralph Meeker. Meeker had been a rising talent in the previous decade, having starred in the original Broadway production of *Picnic* and played Mike Hammer in Aldrich's acclaimed film *Kiss Me Deadly*, as well as starring in Stanley Kubrick's groundbreaking anti-war film *Paths of Glory* (1957). The passage of time was not kind to Meeker, however, and his career had taken a downturn by the time he was cast in his lesser role in *The Dirty Dozen*.

Following Meeker's last scene in the film, "Ralph was overdue to get out of there," Phillips said. "Either it was the end of his contract or he had another engagement. Oh, he also went to a pub with Lee sometimes." It was at that nearby pub that the following incident took place. Meeker's wife, film and stage actress Salome Jens, was with the drunken Meeker. Marvin and Phillips could sense the tension; Phillips recalled that Meeker "had been punching the shit out of her. When Lee and I came into the place, Meeker had already whacked her a couple of times." The bartender simply pointed to the couple and told the two men, "Your mate."

Marvin tried to pacify the couple by asking what was wrong and what could be done. Jens said she was leaving Meeker. Phillips took her outside and told her he would take her to where she was staying. She told Phillips she would take the first plane out and asked if they could keep Meeker at the pub for some time. Phillips returned to the pub, and, as he later recalled, "Now, I don't know if you know what English pubs are like, but they got the sidebar and the pub's on the corner. They had a big side door. I said to Lee, 'Where the fuck is Meeker?' He said, 'He just ran out. He said he was going to apologize to her,' something like that. I turned and walked out." When he couldn't find Jens, Meeker returned to the pub only to be confronted by Phillips: "Meeker and I went to the same high school in Chicago. Anyway, to make a long story short, that was the end of that marriage. I knew Ralph when I got on *The Dirty Dozen*, and Ralph knew me. When I put him against the wall, he said, 'Bobby, no problem. I don't want any problems.' See, I never hit a woman in my life. I would have killed him."

The majority of the film was in the can by that time, and Phillips's work was completed. He went on to Spain for another project and would continue to get minor film and TV work into the late 1990s, including in such films as John Cassavetes's *The Killing of a Chinese Bookie* (1976). Phillips was offered the opportunity to babysit Marvin on several other film projects, such as *Paint Your Wagon* (1969) and *The Klansman* (1974), in which Marvin had daily drinking contests with Richard Burton. Phillips turned them all down. "They wanted to pay me a flat out salary to go up and babysit him," he said. "No part, just babysit. In other words, they said, 'You're the only guy who can control him.' I said, 'He's his own man. I can't control him. Talk reason to him. You can't tell him he's not going to drink. The man's been an alcoholic. The man's got a problem, and he's going to drink. You might be able to sober him up when the show's over, but you're not going to sober him up during the show.' They said, 'You can give him all kinds of advice,' this kind of stuff. I said, 'I don't lead Lee's life, and he doesn't lead mine. I wouldn't do that to him.' I said, 'How do you think I could justify my being there?' They offered me pretty good money, more than I would have made as an actor. Once again, it would have been one step more away from the image I was trying to create of myself as an actor."

Phillips continued to work as an actor into the late 1990s, and earned an Emmy nomination for an episode of *Mission: Impossible*. He took the story of the incident with Meeker and Jens to his grave, requesting it not to be told while he was alive. He passed away in 2018 at the age of ninety-two.

Still yet to be shot on *The Dirty Dozen* was the entire nighttime sequence at the château. The construction of the château caused numerous headaches for Aldrich. Ultimately, it would also become one of the most controversial scenes in motion picture history.

11

"ALDRICH HAD A LOT MORE BALLS"

What began in the spring of 1966 and crawled into the summer eventually slogged into the autumn. The sloth-like pace of *The Dirty Dozen*'s principal photography had frustrated director Robert Aldrich to no end. Exasperated, he took it out on producer Ken Hyman, as can be seen in this August 1966 letter: "Well, we have finally succeeded in doing it. We have at long last topped ourselves in one monumental, monstrous, expensive foul-up that now makes any of our previous misadventures seem minor and insignificant in comparison, namely we've been ready to commence night work at the château for the last 3 days and I'm informed that it will not be ready for us for at least another 2 days, possibly 3, and the ludicrous, farcical fill-in work that we have been doing, in a sophomoric attempt to disguise the obvious, is exactly that, ludicrous. Two days ago, we were working with one actor and one day player. Yesterday we were working with 2 actors and one day player. Today, we were working with 2 actors and a bit player, and in doing so we are leaving the other 12 actors of our cast unused, on salary and living allowance, letting costs uselessly continue to mount, and not only this, we're using up valuable and simple cover sets."

Although the sky above England had finally cleared toward the end of summer, Aldrich's frustration concerning the château's construction was understandable. The initial instructions from Aldrich to veteran art director W. E. "Bill" Hutchinson were as follows: "Build a large French château with a boathouse and bomb shelter connected to tunnels. Include river, landscaping, and garden. We'll use it for 25 nights, then blow it up." Hutchinson and his crew of eighty-five had their work cut out for them.

Rivaling anything else ever built for a motion picture set, the château took more than four months to construct. It was 240 feet long, making it almost the length of an entire football field. It also measured fifty feet high, equivalent to a five-story building. Over two hundred tons of earth were moved to build the château and the six-hundred-foot-long "river" that wound around and past the château. Construction required six hundred thousand feet of lumber, seventy tons of cement, one hundred tons of plaster, eight thousand courtyard cobblestones, and thirty thousand feet of pipe scaffolding with twelve thousand individual fittings.

When it came to landscaping the monstrosity, the numbers were equally monumental. Golf course–smooth grass was needed for the landscape surrounding the château, and gardeners supplied 5,400 square yards of heather, 450 assorted shrubs, 400 ferns, 30 thirty-foot spruce trees, and 6 full-grown weeping willows from MGM's nursery. Adding to the cost was a full-time crew of six who mowed the grass and trimmed the hedges. Making sure it could all be seen in the right light required hundreds of arc lamps and supplemental lights that consumed twelve thousand amps, enough to supply a town of three thousand residents. Powering them were forty-three miles of electric wire.

Bill Hutchinson's son, Tim, was his assistant and recalled, "The château had to have sections of it pre-built in the plans [so] that when it exploded, the front of it, over the door, the balcony, all sort of came away with the explosion, [and] it had to look convincing."

The enormity of the project resulted in an unforeseen set-back. According to Bill Hutchinson, "It wasn't until we were nearly through with construction that the special-effects people told us that our structure was too good and would require seventy tons of explosives to destroy. As a result, we had to rebuild the middle section of the château out of a special foamed plastic and cork. This enabled special effects to blow everything up with only one ton of explosives." This being before the days of CGI, it was no wonder that Aldrich was frustrated. Adding to the problems, according to Jim Dow-dall, "Well, the château was partly destroyed by fire when some kids got into the lot one night set it alight. They had to rebuild part of the set just so that they could blow it up again."

Exacerbating the frustration was the occasional infight-ing that occurred among the cast during the overlong shoot. Englishman Colin Maitland got on the bad side of Clint Walker: "I can remember Clint Walker losing his temper at me when I challenged his politics. Bad decision! Don't argue with someone who's six-foot-six and all muscle!" Asked the nature of the disagreement, Maitland recalled, "I believe it was over the various anti-segregation marches and demonstrations tak-ing place in the southern US at that time. I was very enthusi-astic about ending segregation and wanted the US government to use troops to back up the demonstrators, Clint less so. Not that he was racist, merely that he felt the situation would 'settle down and common sense prevail,' while I doubted segregation would ever end if the government didn't act forcefully."

Ernest Borgnine wrote in his autobiography of an uncomfortable moment he witnessed involving his old friend and comrade Lee Marvin. Borgnine's scenes were scheduled around the hiatus in shooting *McHale's Navy* in the summer of 1966, and, as he wrote, "We were rehearsing one day and we got through with my stuff, so Aldrich called to have Jim Brown brought onto the set. Lee said, 'Yeah, bring in the nigger.' Well, there was a long silence, and then Aldrich said to Lee, 'Would you mind stepping into my office for a moment?' Lee was feeling pretty good and he said, 'Sure.' The two of them went to the small production office in the corner of the soundstage. They came out about ten minutes later. Lee was absolutely sober from that minute forth. Never a demeaning word or anything on his breath when he was working. I don't know if Jim ever heard about what Lee said. Probably not. The former football star was not someone you wanted to cross."

The cast member who proved the most problematic during the long shoot was singer Trini López. The stories of what transpired around his abrupt departure were as varied as the descriptions of an elephant given by the five blind men of fable. They all touch different parts of the animal, and each proclaims it to be something other than an elephant. In the case of Trini López, the versions vary, but they all include Frank Sinatra.

López himself recalled, "The picture was running really, really late. My contract was for four months. I stayed three extra months, and the picture wasn't even half completed. Frank Sinatra was in London. I invited him to dinner, and he said, 'I understand that your film is really running late.' I said, 'Yes, they are.' He said, 'Y'know, you're really hot with your career, and the public is very fickle. I think they'll forget about you. I think you should go back to your career.' I said, 'Do you mean I should leave the film?' He said, 'Yes.'" López failed to mention that, being under contract at Reprise Records, which Sinatra owned, Sinatra was also his boss. Nor did he mention the bad blood that existed between Sinatra and Aldrich after they'd worked together on the disastrous *4 for Texas* (1963).

According to Jim Brown, "The flavor of the month was Trini López. Trini had just released the giant hit 'Lemon Tree.' After we would film, Trini would be surrounded by teenage English girls. In the movie Trini played the part of Jiminez, the little Mexican guy whose comrades berated him at the start but was later to emerge as a hero, diving on a grenade, saving the lives of his fellow Dozen.

"Trini's success was making his head fat. . . . Sinatra told Trini to demand a larger part. If he didn't get it, Sinatra advised, just leave. Trini went back to Aldrich and threatened to walk out if his part wasn't pumped up. He said Sinatra was right behind him. Sinatra in fact said Trini deserved a bigger part. What Trini didn't comprehend was the nature of Bob Aldrich. Bob was one of the few directors in Hollywood with the mind and the balls to handle a gang like ours."

Author E. M. Nathanson also heard a version of what happened: "It was that he had an offer of a job somewhere, a gig—a well-paying gig. I think it was Frank Sinatra who advised him to take it. And other people did. He finally went to Bob Aldrich and said he had to go. He had been kept on longer than he'd planned anyhow. He said he had to leave, so he went. Then I heard two things after that. Let me tell you how it was solved. It was solved when the guys were coming out of the woods or wherever they were, and they look up and they see—we don't even see—what's in the trees. They shake their heads. Then one of them in the dialogue to Reisman says, 'Jiminez got hung up in the tree,' or whatever he says. I heard, or I read it somewhere in recent years [that López] wanted to get back onto the picture the next day, the day after he quit, and Aldrich wouldn't let him. Now, whether that's true or not, I don't know."

Donald Sutherland also had a version. He said, "So [Lopez] came back to Bob Aldrich and said, 'I'm done. I'm finished. You've gone over your time, I'm done.' Trini then came to the screening that night, even though he was done. He looked at the picture and he said, 'Oh shit! Mr. Aldrich, I would like to come back and play it, and finish the role.' Aldrich said, 'You're hanging in a tree, Trini. You're outta here.'"

The way it played out for most involved was explained by Colin Maitland: "So we all showed up for the scene in the forest, and we're waiting around and noticed there's eleven of us. Where's Trini? Finally somebody shows up and whispers into Bob Aldrich's ear. More consultations going on. Finally it's announced to us that Trini has pulled out of the movie and we're going to have to rewrite that scene."

Yet another version was recently retold by a close associate of the late Telly Savalas, who was fond of telling anecdotes from his career. "While filming *The Dirty Dozen*," the anonymous source recalled, "an actor had been cast at the studio's insistence, [and he gave] director Aldrich attitude and exhibit[ed] diva behavior on the first few days of filming. As they wrapped the shoot at the end of one particularly fraught day, Aldrich turned to the scriptwriter and his assistant and hissed, 'Kill him tomorrow!'"

Savalas's version, like the others, may have had some kernel of truth, but it doesn't explain why a writer was on location instead of being contacted to rewrite the scene. In any event, López was indeed ingeniously written out of the film just before the finale at the château. The last script revision, dated August 18, 1966, includes the dialogue stating exactly what happened to Jiminez. In an interesting twist of irony, the singer famous for his hit about a lemon tree was explained to have had his neck broken during the parachute jump . . . by getting hung up in an apple tree.

The grueling pace of the shooting schedule and château construction were ongoing headaches for Aldrich and the company. However, a bright spot did appear in the vacancy left behind by Trini López. Actress Dora Reisser came on set to play the small yet pivotal role of the unnamed victim of Telly Savalas's Archer Maggott. "I got on very well with the whole cast," recalled Reisser. Reisser's life story bore ironic parallels to *The Dirty Dozen*. Born in Sofia, Bulgaria, in 1942, she and her Jewish family survived the Nazi hordes and avoided being shipped to Auschwitz by hiding out for the duration. The experiences she endured in Europe made Reisser a true survivor with driving ambition. Her love of dance led to a solo career with the Venice Opera—that is, until an accidental fall in her late teens ended her dreams of dancing. She changed her focus to acting, learned English, and enrolled at the Royal Academy of Dramatic Arts, where she excelled. While there, she also met her future husband, actor David Weston.

"Jennie Reisser—no relation—the casting director, saw my final performance at the Royal Academy of Dramatic Art," recalls Reisser about getting the role in *The Dirty Dozen*. "I went to the MGM studio at Elstree, met Bob Aldrich, and he straightaway explained what I had to do." Asked her thoughts on working with Aldrich and his all-male cast, she warmly recalled, "The entire Dirty Dozen behaved like gentlemen

Eighteen-year-old Pfc. Lee Marvin overseas during WWII in the Pacific.
(Author collection.)

The entire cast of *The Dirty Dozen* at the initial script reading in England.
Clockwise from the bottom left are: Charles Bronson (Joseph Wladislaw),
Richard Jaeckel (Sgt. Clyde Bowren), George Kennedy (Maj. Max Armbruster),
Trini Lopez (Pedro Jiminez), Al Mancini (Tassos Bravos), Bob Phillips (Cpl. Carl Morgan),
Jim Brown (Robert T. Jefferson), Donald Sutherland (Vernon Pinkley), John Cassavetes (Victor Frank
Ralph Meeker (Capt. Stuart Kinder), Robert Webber (Gen. Francis Denton), director Robert Aldrich
Lee Marvin (Maj. John Reisman), Ernest Borgnine (Gen. Sam Worden), Telly Savalas (Archer Magge
Robert Ryan (Col. Everett Dasher Breed), Clint Walker (Samson Posey), Colin Maitland (Seth Sawye
Ben Carruthers (Glenn Gilpin), Stuart Cooper (Roscoe Lever), unidentified, and Tom Busby (Milo Vlad
(Author collection.)

Producer Ken Hyman (left) and director Robert Aldrich (right)
discuss a scene away from the cast and crew.
(Courtesy Ken Hyman.)

Lee Marvin (left) and Ken Hyman (right) practice the stick fighting skills explained by former self-defense instructor Bob Phillips (center). *(Courtesy Ken Hyman.)*

Telly Savalas (left) and
producer Ken Hyman (right)
in the studio.
(Courtesy Ken Hyman.)

Charles Bronson and
Ken Hyman on location.
Bronson signed the photo,
"To Ken—Your only friend—Charlie."
(Courtesy Ken Hyman.)

Bob Phillips (left), agent Meyer Mishkin (center), and Lee Marvin. *(Author collection.)*

Author E. M. "Mick" Nathanson (center) visits the chateau set and poses with Robert Aldrich (left) and Lee Marvin (right). *(Courtesy Michael E. Nathanson.)*

b Phillips (left),
unidentified friend
m Chicago (center),
l Lee Marvin.
cording to Phillips,
ell'em it ain't coffee
those cups."
uthor collection.)

Dirty Dozen armorer
and later stuntman,
Jim Dowdall,
as a German soldier
on a motorcycle
(which he now owns)
at the back of the set on
first *Dirty Dozen* sequel.
(Courtesy Jim Dowdall.)

"Wolfgang? Wolfgang?" Actress Dora Reisser, who falls prey to crazy Telly Savalas,
reunited with Lee Marvin in Israel in 1985 on the set of *Delta Force*.
(Courtesy Dora Reisser.)

toward me. I watched them play softball in Hyde Park. But the person I really admired was Lee Marvin."

Her opinion of Marvin was quite different from that of the general public. "Lee Marvin, contrary to his screen image, was a gentleman of the old school. He even took my Dalmatian dog for a walk. He cared about the small people in general. I will give you two examples. Once he was called to the set on a wrong day. I asked him if he complained. 'What for? To put the poor girl in trouble?' Another time his limousine arrived and another actor standing close by demanded, 'Where's my limousine?' Lee turned and said, 'Take mine.' I'm giving you just two examples, but that was his attitude to life."

When it came to the role she was required to enact, she recalled how the director explained it: "He took me aside and told me the story of the movie. My part was an easy, good-time girl." However, the role naturally brought back some very unpleasant memories for her. "Until my sons were born, I often had nightmares of being chased through the woods by German soldiers with dogs, so I had a whirring feeling in my stomach when I walked onto the set for the first time and was confronted with hosts of German uniforms. But I had a good director, and I was a good actress. . . . I loved Bob and his German wife, Sam. He was a very powerful director. When he came on the set, even the tough guys were quiet. He created an atmosphere of mutual respect. When I went to LA, because I spoke German I was a frequent guest at their home." Following her brief acting career, she created her own line of popular women's clothing in England and eventually retired with her husband, David.

As the château neared completion, assistant art director Tim Hutchinson recalled, "I think the shoot around the château was probably around fourteen to fifteen weeks, something like that, from the riggers going in and the parts to be seen on top. Though the château was only to be seen at night, it didn't mean that the finish in any way was made easier because of that. You know, the finish still had to be made to look very good."

Apparently, it was when E. M. Nathanson and his family were invited to the set that the château was completed. "The film people were very nice to me," Nathanson recalled. "I'd gotten in touch with Aldrich. He gave me one executive to shepherd me around. We wound up staying around one night when they were shooting the château stuff—not with all the explosions but scenes prior to that. That was mostly standing around waiting, waiting, waiting." Upon seeing the structure big as life, Nathanson said, "The château itself, the construction of it . . . When I came on the set, stumbling over cables and almost banging into trailers, came out into the open and looked up, saw the château and the moonlight was rising over the horizon, I said, 'God, wow!'"

The author's son, Michael, a future author himself, was also there and remembers it from a youngster's point of view. "I was young, maybe not quite thirteen," recalled Michael. "I remember getting to see some of the daily viewings, and also the impressive château facade that was ultimately blown up with quite a bit of strategically placed dynamite for the climax. We were able to hang out with some of the actors as they were on breaks in a trailer, jumping in and out of a running card game.

"I remember my only starstruck moment was talking with Lee Marvin. At one point he had to go to his personal trailer and do something to get ready for the next scene, and he said in his gruff manner, 'Come with me, kid.' He had a son about my age who was about to have a birthday, and he wanted to pick my brain about what electric guitar kids my age would like. At the time, Rickenbacker guitars were the thing that the Beatles had popularized." If Chris Marvin did indeed get that guitar, he has Michael Nathanson to thank, although he ultimately preferred playing the drums.

When it came to the climax of the film, Mick Nathanson was impressed with what Aldrich and company had in mind. He said, "Now, you might say the burning of the guests at the château is no better, as that wasn't in my novel at all. I must say that Aldrich had a lot more balls to put that on screen than I did to put it in the novel."

At the opposite end of the spectrum was John Cassavetes's opinion. "Yeah, I liked it," he said of the film overall. However, he was quick to add, "I didn't like the ending. I tried to ditch out of the ending, actually. I copped out, pretended I was sick, and wouldn't step forward anymore. Bob threatened to sue me! He said, 'You get there and you do what I say.' I just didn't care for killing ninety million Nazis stuck in a basement, throwing a bomb in and burning them up alive. I didn't care for that very much. I didn't see what that had to do with acting."

In filming her horrific scene with Telly Savalas, Dora Reisser had an interesting remembrance. "My part was made bigger, and I was asked to film some more shots," she recalled. "John Cassavetes asked me out of the blue, 'How much are you being paid?' I'm not sure now, but it was between two hundred and five hundred pounds. John said 'Dora, phone Ken Hyman and tell him you want double for the extra shots, and if you don't do it, I will never speak to you again.' I respected John. I phoned Ken Hyman. I got my money." As for her scene's costar, she had praise for Savalas as well: "He was the most charming, intelligent man. He was the first one after he had seen the rushes to come to me and tell me I was great."

Principal photography was finally nearing completion by

mid-October. Clint Walker found himself rather disappointed with the choices Aldrich and Hyman made. He recalled an aspect of his role that he had rehearsed for some time. "I was supposed to do a rain dance," recalled the late actor in the early 1990s. "Bob Aldrich was a football fan, and I think I lost some of what I was supposed to do in order to give Jim Brown a bigger part. I think that was Bob's idea. Of course, Jim was noted for his ability to run. Well, I was disappointed because I practiced for the rain dance. I was looking forward to doing that. In the original script, I was supposed to do a rain dance. Anyhow, it was cut, and that happens."

On the plus side, when Walker wasn't needed on set, he amusingly recalled, "They had me give trophies to the Beatles and the Rolling Stones and all these people. In fact, what amazed me was [that] all those people were so small. Anyhow, I had to be there while they played, and of course they had people on the balconies and so on. They were stomping and screaming and yelling. I thought the building was going to come down!"

When it came time to shoot the standout scene in which Jim Brown runs through the château courtyard dropping grenades down the ventilator shafts, he made a request of Aldrich. "I do remember one scene where I told him I should do something. I should probably get a chance to kill one German, one more German. So, he gave me a scene where I shot one of them off the roof, something like that. I did ask for that, and he gave it to me." As for the controversy of enacting such a scene, the former fullback thought humorously, "It was very interesting to me, because I used to laugh at myself. Here we are, heroes, and I'm dropping grenades on these old German couples and burning them up. I'm thinking this is kind of vicious. But nobody's looking at it that way. They're going, 'Go, Jefferson!' and I'm dropping the grenades. I thought that was a great statement on war, because here we are fighting the enemy and yet these Germans are down there socializing. They're human beings, and I'm dropping bombs and blowing them up."

The reality of that scene is something Capt. Dale Dye found unconvincing: "You've got fragmentation hand grenades, yet when they detonate, you get this huge fireball that looks like a miniature nuclear explosion. These things go off in a quick flash and then a puff of black smoke if you see it in the daytime. What it is [is] that directors think it won't print on film, so they put gas bags in the explosions. They make grenades do a whole hell of a lot more than they actually do. A grenade is designed to scatter shrapnel, small pieces of metal from the casing and the interior, and that causes casualties.

"Another interesting thing to me is a bit off-topic. If you look throughout this film, the Germans, without exception, [aside from] one who's a sentry, there's not a young German in this. Why? Because all of these are old European stunt guys that they hired. Look at the difference in the ages."

Also bothersome to Dye were the historical inaccuracies introduced in service to cinematic convention. "German scopes being red is nonsense. A lot of light in the courtyard is a major mistake. It's a major movie convention. One of the first things I would do is blow those lights out. The director of photography would not let you do that. He needs to have light sources. People would think the scope was infrared, and that's nonsense. The Dirty Dozen not caring about killing women makes sense, but may have ruined [the film's] Oscar chances. Frankly, I wouldn't care much. . . . Walker's detonator box wasn't used at all in the 1940s. . . . [The] vehicle Franko finds *is* a German vehicle. Some of the trucks coming up the road, I have no idea what those are. They look like maintenance vans to me. Again, that's the producer and director saying, 'Nobody knows, and nobody cares.' Jim Brown's M3A1 is notoriously inaccurate. You couldn't hit a bull in the ass with a bass fiddle with this thing, somewhere within fifty meters. Yet they do all of this snap shooting, and they never extend the stock or put it to their shoulder or use the sights."

Despite such obvious problems for him, Dye admits, "I've had a lot of criticisms about *The Dirty Dozen*, technical things. But I think the important aspect here to understand is that it's entertainment, and it's from a different era. It has its own interest and it has its own value in that regard."

In blowing up the château, Colin Maitland recalled, "I will always remember where the big blow-up is to happen. There must have been half a dozen cameras there. Arriflexes everywhere! Robert Aldrich said, 'All right, look, you guys: When this thing goes up, I want you to flinch. I want you to look. It's supposed to be a big explosion.' Well, we didn't have to act at all. They set so many explosives in the thing that when it went up, we nearly dove under a rock to get away from this thing. Boy, did it blow up!" Adding to the cast's reaction, Ken Hyman remembered, "We were about twenty-five miles outside London, and London heard the boom. Lots of complaints from neighbors." Actor Stuart Cooper recalled, "Bob had these huge white cards, and he wrote on the cards all the various pieces of action in the château sequence. I don't know how many cuts are in it, but it's huge."

Interestingly, in the scene that precedes the exploding of the château, when Jefferson shoots Maggott, Jim Brown recalled his costar's reaction in his memoir. "Telly felt he was the star of the movie. When his character, Maggott, got killed, Telly told me, 'Well, Maggott got killed. This movie is over. No one is gonna want to see the rest of it.' And Telly did nail that psychopathic part."

Charles Bronson, brooding and eager to get back to California to be with his bride-to-be, Jill Ireland, was forced to wait a little longer. The final shot was the one in which Lee Marvin drives a huge half-track over the bridge and through a German scout vehicle to escape from the burning château, with Bronson, Richard Jaeckel, and John Cassavetes riding along and firing machine guns. The problem was, Marvin was nowhere to be found.

Producer Ken Hyman drove to London to find him—specifically, to the Star Tavern in Belgravia, which, curiously, was the same pub in which Bruce Reynolds, Ronnie Biggs, and company planned the Great Train Robbery. "Lee was hanging on at the end of the bar, apparently as drunk as a skunk," Hyman later said. "Now, he's the man who has to drive that vehicle across the bridge. I get him into the car and feed him like a child from a flask of coffee. We arrived on the set and got out of the car. Bronson was standing at the back of the château where he'd been waiting for Marvin to show. We pulled in, and Lee sort of fell out of the car. Charlie says, 'I'm going to fucking kill you, Lee!'" Hyman pleaded with Bronson: "Don't hit him, Charlie! Please don't punch him in the face!"

Incredibly, the scene was completed. "He always came through," said Hyman about the hard-drinking Marvin. "There were several moments in the production when he probably couldn't have articulated his own name, but you'd never know it from the sure way in which he moved."

The end result dutifully impressed many of the participants. According to Colin Maitland, "It is dirty. It is grubby. And it is real. I think that's why it works so well and . . . the film has continued. There's no attempt . . . [you never see] guys knocked down, beaten to a pulp, and [then] climb to their feet with nary a bruise or maybe a dab of blood to remove. If somebody gets knocked down, they're hurt, because that's what happens in real life. And if you get knocked down, you get knocked into a sea of mud. You don't fall into a nice, gentle bit of grass. That's why the film works so well, I think."

Principal photography on *The Dirty Dozen* was officially completed on October 16, 1966. The hard work by all involved elicited a huge metaphorical sigh of relief. The premiere was set for June 15, 1967, at New York's Capitol Theater. Until then, what lay ahead was a massive publicity campaign and months of scrutiny dedicated to Robert Aldrich's unique editing of a very unique film.

12

"ALL THOSE MISERABLE
LONG NIGHTS AND DULL DAYS
WERE WORTH IT"

Actor Lee Marvin had planned a long fishing vacation when his work was done, but his plans changed. An enthusiastic young British filmmaker named John Boorman was interested in making a film with his favorite American actor. Boorman discussed his idea for the film *Point Blank* with Marvin at the end of the filming of *The Dirty Dozen* and found a receptive audience. They maintained contact with each other after Marvin returned home to Southern California and worked out the details with the executives at MGM. The one-two combination punch of releases in 1967 would help make Marvin the number-one male box office star in the country.

Robert Aldrich flew back to the States in late October of 1966. Before returning to California, he stopped off in New York to discuss *The Dirty Dozen* with MGM's Robert O'Brien. From there it was on to MGM's Hollywood studio in Culver City, where for the next seven months he and his team of editors, headed by Michael Luciano, hunkered down to create a final edit and sound mix of the film.

As he often did on his domestically made films, Aldrich worked with a sort of stock company of creative entities on his projects. While William Glasgow was Aldrich's usual art director and Joe Biroc his cinematographer, the overseas production of *The Dirty Dozen* meant using Edward Scaife to photograph and Bill Hutchinson as art director. When it came to the film's postproduction, Aldrich could hire Frank De Vol for the music and Luciano to edit. Aldrich's logic was simple and straightforward: "Well, you develop a professional shorthand. You say five words and they know what you mean, and they know how you work, and they trust you, and you trust them, and they don't need to worry about being cautious around you."

The logic held true for Frank De Vol as well. "I've done a lot of work with Frank because he almost always knows and does exactly what I want," said Aldrich. "You speak English to some composers and they answer in music. De Vol's a great musician—fast, inventive, and not very expensive. I've worked with some other very talented musicians, but they weren't able to give me the kind of music I needed. The recording, dubbing, and mixing processes cost much too much to allow you to redo them."

As an arranger and composer, Frank De Vol went professionally by the name Devol. He also found plentiful work as a comedic actor under his full name, Frank De Vol. He began in the days of the big bands and worked prolifically as a film composer from the 1950s through the early 1980s, earning four Oscar nominations along the way. As an actor, he's probably most remembered as the sad-faced bandleader Happy Kyne on *Fernwood Tonight*.

Pennsylvania native Michael Luciano started in the 1930s

and met Aldrich while working on the Robert Rossen boxing classic *Body and Soul* (1947), on which Luciano was assistant editor and Aldrich assistant director. When Aldrich became a full-fledged director he hired Luciano to edit, and continued to do so on practically all of his subsequent films. In fact, Luciano's editing of Aldrich's films resulted in four Academy Award nominations in his career and three Eddie Awards from the American Cinema Editors society.

The editing on *The Dirty Dozen* was of course a matter of securing the proper length, but equally important was the tone that needed to be set throughout. As he had pioneered in many of his previous films, Aldrich begins the movie with an important pre-credits prologue that sets the tone and explains the premise of the entire film. It began with an establishing exterior shot of Maj. Reisman arriving at the fictitious Marston-Tyne Prison to witness the execution of Pvt. Enos Gardiner, filmed at an angle from beneath the gallows as the body drops. Disgusted by what he's witnessed, Reisman leaves to the catcalls of the prisoners he passes. The next image is an exterior shot of wartime London, complete with barrage balloons dotting the skyline and a title that says "London, 1944." The following few scenes are used to explain Reisman's mission as he's forced to endure the haranguing of his superior officers, utilizing quick cuts when the conversation becomes heated. The credits then roll over De Vol's dramatic main theme and close-ups of each prisoner as Sgt. Bowren reads off their names and sentences to Reisman.

As a filmmaker, Aldrich had gone from apprentice to journeyman to master craftsman, and nowhere is that more obvious than in *The Dirty Dozen*. High-angle cuts are seen throughout to create a sense of both imprisonment and ominous claustrophobia. There are scenes in which the viewer is peering down into a room, sudden close-ups creating a nearly terrifying effect, and, best of all, slowly mounted cuts that grow in velocity to rival even the best of Hitchcock. Obvious examples include Reisman's prodding of Posey, the capture of Breed's head-quarters, and an unscripted shot of a dangling rope, shown in a quick-cut close-up, that's inadvertently been left outside the château by Reisman as a German sentry walks by. Best of all is Jefferson's grenade run that ignites the château as trapped, helpless Germans desperately try to get at the gasoline-soaked grenades lodged in the ventilator shafts.

These scenes aren't necessarily artfully done to draw atten-tion to themselves, but they are indeed memorable. Mostly, Aldrich and Luciano prefer a straightforward approach to mov-ing the story along. In terms of some of the macabre humor in the film, noted film historian Matt Zoller Seitz wrote as recently as 2016, "Watch how many times Aldrich cuts from a close-up of somebody in pain or fear to a close-up of an onlooker enjoying themselves." He also accurately observed that, com-pared to Aldrich's action, "Modern action films are all motion, often wasted motion that doesn't have any bearing on the story, and much of it tends to be diced into two-second chunks and amped up by deafening sound effects, which is what directors do when they can't actually direct. . . . *The Dirty Dozen* is built of close-ups and two-shots of craggy-faced actors talking, often softly." The framing of the scenes is equally notable. During the so-called Last Supper celebration before the mission, it's no accident that Reisman is like Jesus at the center of the dais, while Maggott is seated in the same place as Judas.

The editing process resulted in the four hours of the film being seamlessly cut down to two and a half hours. As that pro-cess was taking place, so was the pre-publicity campaign to help build excitement for the film's release. When the paperback version of Nathanson's original novel was published just prior to the film hitting theaters, it proved an impressive barometer of what to expect. When the book was first published in hardcover by Random House, it was also chosen as a Literary Guild selection. According to Nathanson, "Well, it wasn't a big seller. It was if you throw in the Literary Guild deal. Then it sold a few hundred thousand copies. But in paperback, it was a very big seller. It was at least two million copies in this country, and worldwide probably closer to four million."

The author had been to the screening of the film's first rough cut when visiting London and then again later back in the United States. The author definitely had mixed feelings about what he witnessed on screen. "The first time I saw any of it was in a screening room in London, where I saw a lot of footage," he recalled. "Some of it—much of it—still to be shot, particularly the château stuff. And afterward, I was just in awe of it: 'Wow! Gee, it came out of my little head.'"

While in London he also inquired about the name change of one of his most prominent characters. "He was not called Napoleon White in the movie," recalled Nathanson. "He was called Robert Jefferson. I asked, 'Why would they make a change like that?' I asked one of the executives who was squiring me about the set. He said, 'Oh, we found somebody in the telephone book with that name.' That's a very lame excuse."

Complicating the matter even more was a misunderstanding Nathanson had with Jim Brown. In interviews, Brown had said he read the book and loved the character, especially his name, which at one point was going to be Napoleon Jefferson. The change to Robert T. Jefferson did not please Brown, but Nathanson was unaware of the fact. "When I met the man who played Jefferson, the football player, Jim Brown," the author said, "an executive told me that Brown didn't like the name. So,

I confronted Brown with it. I said, 'I understand you didn't like the name Napoleon White,' which is the character's name in the novel. He looked at me kind of strangely and said 'I dunno' [*laughs*]. He didn't know what I was talking about."

When he finally watched the film in its entirety, he was not as pleased. "I remember the first full screening that I saw," Nathanson said. "It was at the MGM studio in Culver City. Russ Meyer was sitting across the aisle from me. When the movie was over, we turned to each other and I went, 'Blech!' and he nodded [*laughs*]. On the way out, I said something to Bob Aldrich like, 'You did it again, Bob!'" It took some time for him to change his mind: "I thought it was an awful picture that would not make a . . . It was really . . . the second time I saw it . . . I had to see it three times before I settled down and really appreciated it as a movie. Now, [at] that first screening in Culver City, it still wasn't complete. There was still some editing and inserts needed to do."

He quibbled about the character of Reisman looking older than he'd intended, but he did like the way Lee Marvin played the part. He also was disappointed in the excising of Tess Simmons as Reisman's romantic interest. "That was a very humanizing part," he said, then added understandingly, "Of course, backstories are sort of the enemy of action films. There was so much in [the book] that they couldn't get on screen." By the third completed screening of the film in general release, he had completely changed his mind and enjoyed it for the pure entertainment value it offered to audiences and himself alike.

The buzz the film generated had a most unusual effect on Nathanson. The years he'd spent researching any and all factual aspects of the story Russ Meyer had told him were for naught, resulting in a work of fiction. However, once the film garnered some prerelease word of mouth with the accompanying book sales, Nathanson remembered, "Other people said, 'Oh yeah. I remember a group like that.' After the book came out and the movie came out, I got photographs of people out in the wilderness. One was a former photographer, maybe a cameraman too, with the army. One was a radio operator. He wrote to tell me that he was the radio operator on the plane that dropped these guys."

The most prevalent rumor he encountered still exists to this day. "Another one sent me pictures that were fuzzy, you know? Fuzzy, these guys just lying around on the airfield with their packs and their helmets, and he said, 'That was the Dirty Dozen.'" The story Nathanson kept hearing after the fact concerned what would later be dubbed the so-called Filthy Thirteen, named by writer Arch Whitehouse in *True* magazine. According to Nathanson, "Then there was another set of pictures of guys in their parachute outfits, mohawk hairdos, camouflage paint, getting ready to board a plane, and one guy wrote me and said, 'That was the Dirty Dozen' [*laughs*]. So here, there, there, widely separated by hundreds of miles in England at that time."

The legend of the Filthy Thirteen still exists, as two of the most celebrated members of the 101st Airborne wrote memoirs of their actions in WWII. One was a Ranger and paratrooper named Jack Womer, and the other was Jake McNiece, a paratrooper with the 101st Airborne combat squad's 506th Parachute Infantry Regiment. In fact, a documentary about McNiece in which he reminisces about not shaving, wearing war paint, and maintaining a mohawk accompanied the DVD release of *The Dirty Dozen*.

At the start of the documentary, Nathanson reminds viewers that McNiece and others were not the Dirty Dozen, since he discovered them *after* the book came out. The rumor still persists, despite the following obligatory disclaimer at the end of the documentary: "While some sources suggested a historical basis for the individuals who allegedly comprised the 'Filthy Thirteen,' there is no connection between any actual persons, living or dead, and the characters portrayed in the fictional motion picture *The Dirty Dozen*. Any similarities between a character in *The Dirty Dozen* and any actual person is entirely coincidental and unintentional."

Other rumors began to arise before the film's release, and some are still stubbornly espoused. Legendary filmmaker Roger Corman believes one of his own low-budget films was responsible for *The Dirty Dozen*. The film was *The Secret Invasion* (1964) and starred Mickey Rooney, Stewart Granger, Raf Vallone, and others as criminal masterminds recruited to abduct a scientist from the Nazis. "The odd thing about this movie is that it had a similar plot to an old western of mine, *Five Guns West* [1955]," recalled Corman. "It also came out before *The Dirty Dozen*. I've heard stories that the producers of *The Dirty Dozen* actually postponed production of their film an entire year because they realized our storyline was similar."

Actually, the premise of bad guys doing good things, especially against Nazis, predates Corman's films—for example, there were WWII comedies featuring the Bowery Boys (known then as the East Side Kids) comically taking on the Germans during the war. There were also several Humphrey Bogart gangster films like *All Through the Night* (1942) and *Passage to Marseille* (1944), in which he's a Devil's Island escapee helping the Free French fight the Nazis. Clearly, some rumors refuse to die. As Jonathan Swift wrote, once famously said, "A lie can travel halfway around the world before the truth can get its boots on."

The rumor mill wasn't confined to the general public. Cast members started their own rumors based on what they were seeing in the dailies. Clint Walker's daughter, Valerie, remembers her father telling her, "In the scenes where they were running toward the camera, a lot of the actors were actually tripping the [others] so they could get their own face forward at the time.

"And he said some had actually paid off the editing room. Dad originally had a much larger role, but they paid off the [editors] in the . . . cutting room to cut Dad's part down. So, it was a pretty competitive thing. Dad, to his credit, didn't do any of that. He felt it was wrong, and he was willing to go ahead and sacrifice whatever happened in the movie and just do a good movie, but that was Dad. He kind of paid the price there, but that was his choice, and I'm proud of him for it." It's an understandable assumption to make about bribing the editor, but hardly likely in light of the relationship between Aldrich and Luciano.

MGM's publicity department was no better when it came to embellishing stories. The pressbook for the film contained ad campaigns, promotional material, and interesting articles for the media to reprint. One such article was entitled "All These Males Ignore Only Girl in Movie's Cast" and humorously describes how Dora Reisser couldn't get any of the male cast members to give her the time of day. Referring to her as a "blonde Bulgarian bombshell," it went on to say Lee Marvin was too busy reading scripts, Jim Brown was plotting his future film career, Clint Walker was exercising, and the rest of the cast was too busy playing poker. Asked about this, Reisser was incensed. "The whole thing is utter nonsense," she responded. "I have never said anything like that. It is beneath my dignity and intelligence. 'Bombshell'! What a joke. The whole thing is a fabrication. I am shocked to be falsely defamed in this manner."

Probably even more creative were some of the promotional

ideas MGM dreamed up for local theater owners. They included promoting the Dell comic book adaptation and the soundtrack album, which was nothing compared to some of the more whimsical ideas. There was a contest for the local radio station for listeners to come up with as many movie titles with the number twelve or just with numbers in the title as possible. There was a suggestion to hold a late-night "Commando Screening" featuring prizes for anyone showing up in camouflage clothing. Another idea was to come up with twelve ways to bake a cake or wash a car and tie them in with a local bakery or car wash. The most bizarre notion was a giveaway of toy hand grenades tied to a local toy store.

There was a separate promotional section entitled "Interest the Ladies." Some of the most extreme examples included promoting a local laundry day for guests who brought in over twelve pounds of laundry! That may be the strangest, but there were some close runners-up, such as babysitter day or getting a local women's store to host a military clothing day.

All these embellishments, fabrications, misconstrued tales, and outlandish ballyhoo swirled while Aldrich was finishing the editing of the film. By February 1966 his work print was shaping up to be quite impressive—so much so that he wrote a group letter to half the cast congratulating them on the nearly finished product. He ended by stating, "So, gentlemen, congratulations. Who knows? Maybe we have a hit on our hands and all those miserable long nights and dull days were worth it. Again, congratulations. Onward and upward."

The reason for the good vibes Aldrich sent out was that good vibes were also received. According to the same memo, "I made up a temporary print with canned music, partial effects, etc., etc. and showed this rough [cut] to about 175 people last week. This group was made up of your American counterparts, some of their agents, a couple of old friends, and a good deal of MGM Culver City personnel. All I can tell you is the reaction was extraordinary. Perhaps even better than that. And the one single comment that was usually mentioned first was how good the entire cast was."

It was because of such test screenings that Aldrich wrote another memo to Ken Hyman. He wrote, in part, "Don Sutherland is so goddamned good in this picture, and the audiences love him so much and his part is so important, it seems terribly unfair to drop him down with all the other local laborers and slough him off of feature billing. Consequently, I'm suggesting we pull him out of this billing and stick him up alphabetically, which would put him between Savalas and Walker."

Other than Lee Marvin's top billing, the rest of the named cast were indeed listed alphabetically. When asked about his exclusion from most of the advertising, Donald Sutherland recently said, "I have no idea what you're talking about. Did Kenny Hyman do what Mr. Aldrich had requested [he] not [do]? If he didn't, that was because Kenneth wasn't in contact with his father [Eliot Hyman]. His dad was a terrific movie-making man and would have told him to do it. His son, regrettably, didn't get there. Mr. Kenneth Hyman's imagination paled in comparison with Mr. Aldrich's, and that seemed to constantly irk him."

The fact of the matter is that Sutherland was indeed featured in some of the advertising, such as the image of the hand grenade in which the faces of the cast were shown in the grenade's segments. Most likely Hyman heeded Aldrich's advice when he could, based on the timing of the ad campaign's completion. The main poster used for most of the ad campaign was a colorful depiction of scenes from the film, with the likes of Lee Marvin, Charles Bronson, and Jim Brown clearly shown, along with another soldier who may be Telly Savalas, as he has a bald pate but facially looks more like Mr. Clean. The artist was the fairly prolific Frank McCarthy, of James Bond poster fame, and it included the tagline, "Train them! Excite them! Arm them! . . . And then turn them loose on the Nazis!"

The marketing blitz for the film's summer opening was one of saturation. Full-color, full-page ads were readied for such national magazines as *Sports Illustrated*, *Esquire*, *Playboy*, *True*, *Sport*, *Argosy*, *American Legion Magazine*, and *VFW Magazine*. A network short on the making of the film aired on CBS, and a story serialization of the film appeared in *Screen Stories* magazine. Prepared radio interviews with the stars were sent out to radio stations, and editorial breaks were planned for *Life*, *Look*, and all the major national magazines to coincide with the film's release.

When it came to the film's June 15 world premiere at the Loews Capitol Theater in New York, MGM genuinely outdid itself. Press from around the world were invited to join the cast for three days of festivities. It began with an afternoon buffet at the Americana Hotel's Princess Ballroom, followed by a short walk to the theater around the corner. After the premiere, all attendees went to a post-premiere champagne supper and dance at Rockefeller Plaza. Practically the entire cast was in attendance, along with Aldrich and Hyman. Celebrities from the world of show business, politics, business, and sports were also present, such as Celtics star Bill Russell, famed lawyer Louis Nizer, and a host of others. Lee Marvin brought neither his ex-wife nor his girlfriend; instead, he was in attendance with his father, Monte Marvin.

Over the next two days, the gala continued, with MGM picking up the tab for a luncheon at the Sky Room and a supper at Toots Shor's. It concluded with a boat ride around Manhattan that ended up at New Jersey's Monmouth Park racetrack for a featured race in honor of the film. The studio obviously had high hopes for their product. When the confetti finally settled, the reviews were set to make *The Dirty Dozen* one of the most hotly debated films of the decade.

13

"A SPIRIT OF HOOLIGANISM
THAT IS BRAZENLY ANTISOCIAL"

The film's premiere gala proved quite successful and included a reunion of sorts for much of the cast and crew. Since the film premiere was on June 15, the Six-Day War, which had taken place just the week before, was very much in the news. Israel had successfully defended itself against Egypt, Jordan, and Syria in a miraculous six days. Dora Reisser recalled of Lee Marvin at the *Dirty Dozen* premiere, "He admired the Jews, and was a great supporter of Israel, especially the IDF [Israeli Defense Force], our army. The Six-Day War took place, and as a veteran soldier, he marveled at the expertise of the IDF against unimaginable odds. Three million Jews were surrounded by hundreds of [millions of] enemies. Lee told me of his admiration for the IDF whilst I was in New York for the opening."

Reisser and Marvin would meet up again in Israel when he was filming *The Delta Force* (1986), which would be his last theatrical film. They got along like the old friends they were, even though she was no longer acting. She had made a few film and TV appearances but left acting to become one of Britain's most successful fashion designers. She is now happily retired and enjoying life with her husband, children, and grandchildren.

The premiere of *The Dirty Dozen* took place at the Loews Capitol Theater with a dual booking at the 34h Street East Theatre, and the film reaped a combined three-day gross of nearly $70,000. The take continued to make regular headlines in trade papers and mainstream news outlets.

A few weeks after the film's premiere, Robert Aldrich went on a fact-finding mission. In response to comments he was getting calling the film far-fetched and unbelievable, he let it be known that he was going to find proof that there actually was a group of WWII prisoners who had been sent on a secret mission. His first stop was the Army Repository on Long Island, where he believed Russ Meyer's footage might still exist. Like Mick Nathanson, his search came to for naught.

Other events in the news actually correlated to *The Dirty Dozen*. US involvement in Vietnam began to pick up momentum during the Johnson administration, as did opposition to the war. Bombing had resumed when the film was in production, and by the end of 1966, the US death toll had reached over 8,700 soldiers. By October the following year, the casualties were more than 22,000 troops. Anti-war protests were springing up all over the country, with one of the largest taking place at the Pentagon in Washington, DC.

Interestingly, Robert Aldrich had said the original script by Nunnally Johnson was a good script for 1945 but not for 1967, when the film was to be released. The influence of the war's escalation was obvious. Yet after the film was in general release, Aldrich said, "When we planned *The Dirty Dozen* in 1965, do you think for one moment we knew that by the time the film came out the French kids would be in revolt and Americans would be sick of Vietnam, so the mood would be just right for our picture? Rubbish. The fact that the film grossed $80 million was luck. Pure luck." (Earnings were closer to $40 million) He also said, "Fascinatingly, European critics all picked up on the parallel between burning people alive and the use of napalm [in Vietnam], whether they liked the picture or not. They all got the significance of what was being said. So, you learn not to overreact to criticism, whether it's favorable or unfavorable."

European critics had championed the work of Aldrich's films long before their American counterparts. His film *Kiss Me Deadly* was heralded in Europe, while Americans criticized the level of violence portrayed in the nuclear holocaust scenario. Aldrich had always believed that violence in a film did not result in violence in life but the other way around. In a 1955 editorial for the *New York Herald Tribune*, he defended his point of view as criticism swirled around his film even before it was released. He wrote, "If you stripped the elements of violence from both testaments of the Bible and Shakespearean drama, the entire literature of the world would be sorely impoverished. The 'original creative plottings' of all writers have always been influenced by these two masterful resources."

The reviews of *The Dirty Dozen* were decidedly mixed, but one of the first was from the *New York Daily News*, which gave it its highest rating and declared, "Possibly the most unique war drama ever filmed opened last night at the Capitol Theater to the loudest blast of applause ever heard on Broadway." Unfortunately, it would not be a sign of things to come.

The controversy over violence in film reared its ugly head yet again when *The Dirty Dozen* was released. In his review, entitled "Brutal Tale of 12 Angry Men," *New York Times* film critic Bosley Crowther led the charge. The first salvo was fired across the bow in his opening paragraph: "A raw and preposterous glorification of a group of criminal soldiers who are trained to kill and who then go about this brutal business with hot, sadistic zeal is advanced in *The Dirty Dozen*, an astonishingly wanton war film."

He would go on to spew even more negative platitudes, adding, "To bathe these rascals in a specious heroic light—to make their hoodlum bravado and defiance of discipline, and their nasty kind of gutter solidarity, seem exhilarating and admirable—is encouraging a spirit of hooliganism that is brazenly antisocial, to say the least." He would then go on for five more lengthy paragraphs criticizing every aspect of the film's plot, script, direction, and cast. Clearly, the battle lines had been drawn and the war of words had begun.

Aldrich didn't respond in print to Crowther's criticism, but years later he told an interviewer, "You have to feel like a politician. If Crowther knocks you, you're in very good company. And I certainly would much rather have a spirit of 'brazen hooliganism' than what passes for patriotism now."

Other reviewers joined the Crowther chorus by denouncing the very premise of the film, as well as the violence. John Mahoney of the *Hollywood Reporter* bemoaned the grainy quality of the 70 mm print he viewed, believing it was blown up to give the film more importance. He called the attack on the château "immensely cluttered," adding, "Many will be offended that it includes an act by the US team in which they pour grenades and gasoline through air vents onto officers and women trapped in a bomb shelter, incinerating them Buchenwald style." The entire review is decidedly mixed, with some aspects highlighted positively, and poses a question about Bronson's last line, "Killing generals could get to be a habit with me." Mahoney asks rhetorically, "Is that line supposed to ring pacifistically?" Not only a spoiler for the ending but an odd question to pose based on the entire film.

Variety's reviewer, "Murf" (the pen name of Arthur D. Murphy), also took the film's 70 mm print to task, and then raised an interesting question: How does Robert Ryan's character know that prostitutes were brought into the compound by Marvin's character if the entire premise of the film was supposed to be kept top secret? It becomes a valid question, since the subplot concerning Lady Margot had been removed from the film. "Murf" does get wrong the fact that Marvin's character picks the dozen. Marvin states in the film that he did not choose the lineup; the army did. Because *Variety* is a Hollywood trade paper, though, "Murf" ultimately concludes that the film is an "exciting film version of the book. Lee Marvin heads an excellent cast. Overlong but hot box office likely, including femme audience despite all-male principals."

The critic for *Cue* magazine, Jesse Zunser, felt the film was a rousing adventure in the war film genre but asked if there was any true cinematic achievement present. "But what if one hopes for a glimmer of art?" he asks. "Robert Aldrich is all robust energy and bluster in this yeoman adventure. He knows to make the exterior tough, the relationships violent, the inevitable showdown battle noisy and explosive. But he doesn't know how to forgo the easy gag and comic relief, to keep us more rooted in reality." In summary, "you laugh hard and wince hard."

Not all critics jumped on the Crowther bandwagon. Mandel Herbstman of *Film Daily* was much more generous in his review. "War Adventure Told on a Large Canvas with Power and Gusto," read his headline. He then went on to delineate and praise each cast member's character and the overall production, stating, "The drama is hard, savage, and relentless. If there is such a thing as a women's picture, this might well be called a men's picture. It may not appeal to all audiences, but its merits will certainly win a large percentage. Mark it down for strong gross."

The *Motion Picture Herald*'s Richard Gertner questioned the believability of the plot but deemed it worthy, due to the fact he considered Robert Aldrich "a master storyteller with a camera. He does a lot of subtle things in bringing out the characters of the men involved; he introduces humor naturally and engagingly, and builds suspense steadily along the way." In conclusion, he wrote, "It doesn't really feel too long at two and a half hours—packs a wallop and brings the whole business to a smashing close."

Richard Schickel, in his review for *Life* magazine, found the film flawed but highly entertaining, despite the plot being what he considers a largely immoral tale: "Never in the movies have you seen such a thoroughly unpleasant gang of American soldiers engaged in such a thoroughly unpleasant adventure." He also felt the higher-ranking officers in charge were actually more brutal than the dozen in the way they callously have Reisman "volunteer" to train and pursue their mission. His opening summation states his case: "*The Dirty Dozen* is a confused, violent, sometimes tasteless, often exciting movie that, because the motives of its makers are badly mixed, requires patience and fortitude on the part of the audience if disbelief is to be suspended and its potent message apprehended. Flawed as it is, however, it seems to me one of the most interesting films about the brutalizing effects of war that we have had from American filmmakers in the last decade."

The constant mention of the film's box office potential in several reviews is an interesting aside. Some reviewers saw that audiences didn't really care what critics thought and enjoyed the movie for the entertainment value it offered, as well as the intriguing premise and characters. The *Los Angeles Times* posted an article the month after the film came out saying that MGM's third-quarter revenues were the highest it had ever seen in its forty-three-year history, due mainly to the opening of *The Dirty Dozen*. As Mick Nathanson frankly yet accurately stated, "*The Dirty Dozen* really saved MGM's ass."

As the film opened wider throughout the summer in key demographic cities, so too did the grosses. The *Daily Variety* front page headline of August 8 blared, "DIRTY DOZEN CLEANING UP." The article claimed that the film made $7.5 million in its first five weeks of release. Though much of that total was based on its wide release in over a thousand theaters, it's still an extraordinary feat in so short a period of time. MGM's assistant sales chief Herman Ripps, when asked about the film's projected gross, proudly boasted, "In this case, you have to throw the book away." Ripps claimed estimates for domestic receipts could go as high as $25 million. The basis for such astronomical projections was that, at the time of the article, the film had only a few foreign dates planned, with more on the way. When released in more foreign countries, the estimate would skyrocket.

As the film's immense popularity grew, a debate began among some reviewers concerning whether there were anti-war, antisocial, or antiauthoritarian themes inherent in the film.

Writing in the *Christian Advocate*, critic James Wall opined that the film was most definitely anti-war: "This is a violent film, too violent perhaps for anyone under twelve. But it is an anti-war picture, and should be received as such by thoughtful churchmen." It's interesting to note that such a religiously themed periodical would make this pronouncement.

Arthur Knight of the *Saturday Review* skewed the point

by writing, "Indeed, the realization that authority not only has its uses but, for some men, fulfills an aching need is a bitter pill that Aldrich coats with bountiful action, robust humor, and a uniformly superb cast." An anonymous columnist for the *New Yorker* decried the debate over whether the film was anti-war or not. In a lengthy editorial, they pontificated on the lack of courtesy in the world today by describing their terrible experience in attempting to view the film—rude cab-driver, rude usherette, rude patrons, etc., etc. Ultimately all this led them to proclaim, "The film is neither anti-war nor pro-war but merely a replica of war."

An anonymously penned review in the *Canyon Crier* condemned the film entirely, stating, "We consider *The Dirty Dozen* an obscene film." The reviewer then goes on to claim that, in the film, sadism is rampant, racism against Blacks is condoned, and the commanding officers are just as stupid and criminal as the dozen. It makes one wonder whether the reviewer had seen the same film as everybody else.

On the *Today* show, critic Judith Crist gave the film an unabashed rave, saying, "Taking the premise that war is a sport for murderers, criminals, and near madmen, Robert Aldrich has turned *The Dirty Dozen* into one of the best and least compromising he-man adventure films. It's superbly cast, everyone from Lee Marvin down. And thanks to Aldrich, it will keep you on the edge of your seat for about two and a half hours. It's a slam-bang, grown-up adventure story, thumbing its nose at authority and morality and at the compromise that is Hollywood's war cliché. It's cruel and unpleasant on an intellectual level, but that, of course, is war."

Whether calling the film a smash or an immoral bomb, reviewers seem to have missed one crucial aspect that was a compelling reminder of the time in which the movie was released. A mere five days after the film's premiere, boxer Muhammad Ali was found guilty of violating Selective Service laws by refusing to be sent to Vietnam. The case was appealed for years, going all the way to the Supreme Court, where the conviction was unanimously overturned in 1971. In the ensuing years, Ali had his boxing license revoked in his prime while becoming an outspoken defender of civil rights and protests against the war. His logic was direct and powerful: "I ain't got no quarrel with them Vietcong. No Vietcong ever called me nigger."

His friend and former fellow athlete Jim Brown stated emphatically at the beginning of *The Dirty Dozen*, when asked to join the mission to kill Germans, "That's your war, man, not mine. You don't like the Krauts, major, you fight them. Me, I'll pick my own enemies." Different wars, but the message is clear. In a single moment in the film, the rise of the anti-war movement and the rise of the civil rights movement were intertwined as never before, and all in a war film that was analogous to Ali's stance on both the Vietnam War and race relations.

As the long, hot summer of 1967 dragged on, so too did the social upheaval in the nation. Riots had taken place in the Watts neighborhood of Los Angeles in 1965, and by the summer of 1967 more rioting had broken out in Detroit, to be followed by riots in Trenton, New Jersey, in 1968. The basic cause of the civil unrest was the treatment of African Americans by police. The passage of time was not kind to such continued unrest, as the assassinations of civil rights leader Martin Luther King Jr. and presidential candidate Robert F. Kennedy, both in 1968, created major polarization in the country. Following the murders of King and Kennedy, rioting broke out in Chicago, Baltimore, Boston, Cleveland, and Pittsburgh.

The war in Vietnam continued, as did the anti-war protests as a result of both the Tet Offensive and the My Lai Massacre in 1968, all while *The Dirty Dozen* was still playing in theatres. The unprecedented events of the time helped lead to an unprecedented box office take, making *The Dirty Dozen* the number-one film of the year and the highest-grossing film in MGM history at that time. Studio executives slowly began to see the advantage of releasing big-budget films in the summer when kids were out of school and many people went on vacation. The seasonal summer blockbuster became a permanent fixture in movie theaters long before *Jaws* (1975) and remains in effect to this day.

The award season for films released in 1967 began in earnest in 1968, and several groundbreaking films were either nominated or awarded by various organizations. Front-runners included *Cool Hand Luke, Bonnie and Clyde, Guess Who's Coming to Dinner, The Graduate, In the Heat of the Night, In Cold Blood*, and *The Dirty Dozen*. Also, strangely enough, *Doctor Doolittle* was very much in the running. Michael Luciano had won the aforementioned Eddie from American Cinema Editors, and Lee Marvin received a Golden Laurel Award for Best Action Performance. The film also took the Gold Medal at the Photoplay Awards. Those were the wins. Aldrich was nominated for Best Director by the Directors Guild, as was Cassavetes for Best Supporting Actor at the Golden Globes. Cassavetes and Brown were both nominated for Golden Laurel Awards. None of them won.

The Academy Award nominations were to be announced on February 19, 1968, and *The Dirty Dozen* looked to be a shoo-in for several major nominations. Columnist Abe Greenberg wrote in the Hollywood *Citizen-News* that the film was so good that the real dilemma was figuring out who in the cast should be Oscar-nominated. He assumed Lee Marvin was the obvious choice but added a solution for the rest of the cast: "The

Academy might consider the possibility of a new category as the Best All-Star Cast Award! These men deserve it!"

When the nominations were announced, the results were disappointing. There was no nomination for Best Picture, though *Doctor Doolittle* received one. *The Dirty Dozen* received only four nominations, for MGM's Studio Sound Department's sound editing, Michael Luciano's film editing, John Poyner's sound effects, and John Cassavetes in the Best Supporting Actor category. Poyner won, but MGM, Luciano, and Cassavetes finished out of the money in their categories. Ironically, the winner for Best Supporting Actor was George Kennedy, Cassavetes's *Dirty Dozen* costar, for *Cool Hand Luke*.

There was a rumor that Aldrich was denied a Best Director nomination due to the film's violent content, especially its ending. Indeed, in some foreign markets the scene was either excised or edited down, but not in the US. It has been said for years that had Aldrich changed the ending, he would definitely have received a nomination, a conjecture that has been repeated so many times that it's believed to be true.

According to the film's producer, Ken Hyman, it isn't. "I never heard the rumor," he said recently, "and I doubt that it ever existed." Aldrich's not being nominated was probably due more to the mutual lack of interest in each other between him and the Hollywood establishment. Knowing the kinds of films the Academy and the Hollywood establishment preferred, Aldrich once sarcastically noted that he wouldn't get a nomination even if he had directed a biblical epic, which he did with 1962's *Sodom and Gomorrah*.

Fans of *The Dirty Dozen* who know their military history found discrepancies in some of the military procedures. Capt. Dale Dye, who has served as an adviser on many films and TV shows, has a laundry list of issues with the film. "One of the things that bothers me is they've all got steel helmets on," he said. "Look at the light reflected off of those steel helmets. You would not have it. You may jump with the helmet to protect your head, but you would get rid of it. You'd be wearing a soft cap and your face would be tremendously camouflaged, because nothing reflects ambient light like your skin. . . . Why didn't they do it? Because then you can't see the actors! It's just nonsense. I would have made them do it and found a way to make the actors look cool in it, as opposed to doing it this way. These guys, they're not paying attention to the combat elements of this thing."

The film's armorer, Jim Dowdall, was also aware of errors in the film based on the time period. "The inaccuracies were plain to see if one had any kind of basic WWII knowledge," said Dowdall. "The Germans with MP 40s were all fitted with rifle pouches. The 'armored car' pushed by the half-track off the edge of the bridge was a British Daimler Dingo with a ridiculous sort of gunners' platform made of wood bolted onto the top and a German Cross painted on the side. The big truck was a British Bedford QL . . . with the German cross painted on the door. The Bofors gun hooked up to the back of the half-track was very much a British Army piece of equipment, and worst of all, the ambulance used in the scene where George Kennedy is pushed off the side was a Dodge M37 [of the type] used by the US Army from 1951 onward.

"In the war games scene, which we filmed in Aldbury, there is a tracked Jeep TJ Mk1, which is seen crossing from right to left in front of the pond. There were only six of these produced experimentally for the Canadian Army and never adopted. One came to England for trials that were unsuccessful and it never saw the light of day, and certainly not in the US Army. It was owned by Bapty, my employer, and just stuck in to make up the numbers. I could go on, but in those days, as long as all the Germans wore the German helmet, they were the bad guys and nobody bothered about any accuracy on the historical front. *Saving Private Ryan* [1998] was really the first major war film to attempt a real degree of accuracy, although the 'Tiger' was so clearly a Russian T-34 that it was embarrassing. I was the one who drove it in the movie."

14

DIVERGING ALUMNI

The effect the phenomenal success of *The Dirty Dozen* had on those involved was equally phenomenal. Both cast and crew members experienced a major uptick in their careers as a direct result of *The Dirty Dozen*'s box office, and entirely new careers that had a lasting effect on the entire film industry were launched.

For Ken Hyman, it meant being considered the new wunderkind in Hollywood. Warner Bros. studio boss Jack Warner sold his remaining 30 percent stake to Seven Arts, Eliot Hyman's successful independent production company, and the elder Hyman made his then thirty-nine-year-old son Ken head of production at the newly formed Warner Bros.–Seven Arts. "I wasn't a former agent running a studio," Hyman told Sam Peckinpah biographer David Weddle in 1994. "I wasn't a deal maker. I was a hands-on producer, I was a picture maker, and I believed in doing everything I could to support the director, to allow him to make the movie he wanted to make."

Hyman certainly proved that statement by working on set

daily with Robert Aldrich, and he stood by it as studio head by green-lighting such successful, offbeat productions as Paul Newman's directorial debut *Rachel, Rachel* (1968), starring his wife, Joanne Woodward. Hyman gave famed black photographer Gordon Parks his first directing credit with his autobiographical film *The Learning Tree* (1969), based on Parks's own novel. He also helped launch the careers of Paul Mazursky with the offbeat comedy *I Love You, Alice B. Toklas* (1968), as well as that of George Lucas by approving the expansion of his futuristic student film into a feature-length production entitled *THX 1138* (1971). In fairness, not all his executive decisions were good ones, as he passed on William Goldman's script for *Butch Cassidy and the Sundance Kid* (1969), which 20th Century-Fox immediately swooped up.

Hyman redeemed himself in the form of the strange man he had met years before at the Cannes Film Festival following a screening of *The Hill*. "I ended up doing the production thing at Warners," Hyman recently said. "I remember asking somebody in publicity, 'How do I get in touch with a guy called Peckinpah?' They said, 'What do you want to be involved with that drunk for?' I didn't ask them about his character. I just wanted his phone number. I called Sam. I said, 'Mr. Peckinpah, we met at the Cannes Festival, and you liked the movie that I produced called *The Hill*. I'm out here now. Do you want to have a couple of beers?' And I knew he'd say yes."

When they met, Peckinpah proceeded to tell Hyman he had been fired and blackballed for putting a nude woman in the movie *The Cincinnati Kid* (1965). Hyman recalled the result of their meeting: "I said, 'Tell me, what have you got in mind?' He said, 'Well, I got a thing I'm looking to do. Why do you want to know?' He didn't know I was going to be in charge of production at Warners. So I said, 'You were nice about *The Hill* and

I'm trying to be nice and show an interest in your problems.' He said, 'Well, it's called *The Wild Bunch*.'"

Hyman was only slightly impressed at the time, but when he requested rewrites, Peckinpah and his writing partners kept at it until Hyman was fully impressed. Lee Marvin was sought for the lead and very much wanted to do it. However, when Paramount offered Marvin a million dollars for Paddy Chayefsky's scripted version of the musical *Paint Your Wagon*, he went with it, putting an end to his movie winning streak. William Holden was signed for the lead instead. As a small substitute or possibly for luck, *Dirty Dozen* costars Robert Ryan and Ernest Borgnine gave the film strength in secondary leading roles. By the time production began and the dailies came back from the Mexico location, Hyman wired Peckinpah to tell him that despite the costs and difficulties, "Just for the record, *The Wild Bunch* will wind up in history as one of the greatest pictures of all time. Thank you, thank you, and thank you again." Not only was Hyman's prediction right, but when the film was released in 1969, it also proved to be even more brutal and violent than *The Dirty Dozen*.

Paint Your Wagon's failure at the box office and with critics was a noticeable embarrassment for Marvin. At the same time, the biggest buzz in Hollywood surrounded *The Wild Bunch*. Marvin let his sour grapes be known upon viewing the film. According to author David Weddle, "They had a screening at Warners, and Marvin was invited. He showed up totally bombed. During the film, he's shouting out stuff: 'More blood!' 'Aw, c'mon, kill 'em some more, Sam!' One person even said he was crawling down the aisles saying things. Someone finally said, 'Shut up, Lee!'"

For director Robert Aldrich, the success of *The Dirty Dozen* proved to be both a blessing and a curse. He had started his own production company, called Associates & Aldrich for his appreciation of his coworkers, earlier in his career, and as a fiercely independent producer he utilized the company to make the movies he wanted to make. The success of *The Dirty Dozen* allowed him to take that independent streak a step further. He sold his percentage of the film back to MGM for the hefty price tag of $1.5 million and used the money to realize an even greater goal: in January of 1968, he purchased his own private studio.

Located at 201 North Occidental Boulevard in Los Angeles, the property was developed in 1913 and had gone through many owners, such as Mary Pickford and Paramount founder Jesse L. Lasky. Aldrich bought the property from educational and government filmmaker John Sutherland. Aldrich had used the studio on some of his previous films and knew what he could do with it. The price for the purchase and remodeling of the studio was over $1 million, but he saw the studio as a way to not only make the kind of films he wanted but to ensure he could use his regular stable of artists and craftsmen, whom he kept on the payroll. He said, "If, as I suspect, we're entering that last chapter of movie-making in Hollywood itself, I like to think the Aldrich Studios will be there at the finish."

His purpose in buying the studio would also be the reason for its ultimate failure. Keeping people on the payroll whether they were working or not proved costly. Worse, the films that were made there were anything but box office gold. In quick succession, Aldrich directed *The Legend of Lylah Clare* (1968), *The Killing of Sister George* (1968), and *Too Late the Hero* (1970), all deemed critical and commercial disasters.

The films were each too reminiscent of previous films or too cutting-edge for the audiences of the day. Based on a 1963 TV drama, *Lylah Clare* concerned a film director (Peter Finch) obsessed with a starlet (Kim Novak) who bears a striking resemblance to his late actress wife. Ernest Borgnine was cast as a producer who came off as Aldrich's alter ego. Comparisons were made to *Sunset Boulevard* (1950), but not in a good way. *Sister George* was based on a British stage play in which an aging lesbian soap opera star (Beryl Reid) deals with the loss of her career as well as her relationship with a younger woman (Susannah York). Along with *What Ever Happened to Baby Jane?*, it cemented Aldrich's reputation as a cult director in the gay community but was too far ahead of its time for the mainstream.

His other film, *Too Late the Hero*, sought to reclaim the success of *The Dirty Dozen*, just as the Aldrich Studio production *What Ever Happened to Aunt Alice?* sought to emulate the success of *Baby Jane*. *Aunt Alice* starred Geraldine Page as a crazed woman hiring other women as housekeepers, bilking them out of their money, and then killing them. In *Too Late the Hero*, a motley group of British and American forces, led by Michael Caine and Cliff Robertson, attempt to make it back to base through a jungle following a commando mission on a Japanese-held island during WWII. Neither film was a hit, and consequently, Aldrich Studios went bankrupt. Aldrich's next several films as a director suffered similar fates, but the stubborn and independently creative filmmaker couldn't be counted out. He hit his stride once more with a 1974 film perfectly in tune with audiences and critics alike. Not surprisingly, it conveyed themes similar to those in *The Dirty Dozen* but did so much better than *Too Late the Hero*.

Of the other alumni of *The Dirty Dozen* whose careers were affected by the film's monumental success, Donald Sutherland is one of the best examples. In 1991, Sutherland told the *Los Angeles Times* that while he was still in England, "This particular scene had had a lot of success, and . . . I had a big chance to come to California to capitalize on the scene. I had no money. I phoned [fellow Canadian] Christopher Plummer, who was at Stratford at the time, to ask if I could borrow $1,500 to get to the United States. He said it would be at his lawyer's office in the morning."

When Sutherland arrived in Hollywood, he was up for a lead role in Robert Altman's offbeat war comedy *M*A*S*H* (1970), but the director was uncertain of Sutherland's comedic ability. As he had done to get the role of Vernon Pinkley, Sutherland had his agent send Altman some footage that convinced him. The clip was from *The Dirty Dozen*.

The versatile Sutherland is on record as saying that one of his biggest professional disappointments was that he never worked with Aldrich again, although the opportunity was there. Asked what project it was, he said, "*Too Late the Hero*. It conflicted with two films I'd already been committed to: *Kelly's Heroes* [1970] and *Klute* [1971]. Trying to squeeze it in would have meant onerous stop dates and really not enough time to prepare for *Klute*. And also because I was already heading for Yugoslavia with *Kelly's Heroes*; she (his wife) would have left me if I'd gone to the Far East. Ah my, what to do? Decisions, decisions between the film and my wife! Mind you, if I'd been free to go I would have, and she could have come." Asked what his other memories about making *The Dirty Dozen* were, he referred to the experience as group theater and simply said, "Too many, too personal, too painful to dredge up. And I'm not interested in dredging them up!"

Charles Bronson's work in the film helped lay the groundwork for his ascent to international stardom, and may have been the most rewarding trajectory, personally and professionally. Once *The Dirty Dozen* was finished, he was able to properly mourn his mother's passing and reunite with Jill Ireland. They married in 1968 after both their divorces had been finalized the year before. The actor's mood changed considerably following all that transpired in the Aldrich film, but it would still be the last time they would work together. Aldrich had said of Bronson, "Charlie Bronson could have been a great actor, but he's not aware of his own potential and he missed his chance."

Bronson himself didn't hold Aldrich in high regard either. In a rare 1977 interview, he said of Aldrich, "A very good director. Beyond that, he has one fault: he is inflexible. He's horrified if you give him ideas; he only appreciates his own. He wants to use his own brain for everything. That's his greatest fault. If he wasn't so inflexible, he would be very great. He refuses to give in. Well, it's impossible for one man to know everything." His initial thoughts of the film weren't very high either; he claimed to Rex Reed that he walked out of the theater halfway through it. He added, "*The Dirty Dozen* is nothing more than a diversion. It could have been much better, and we knew it as we were filming. The cast was made up of excellent actors and the director was good, but the story wasn't very good. . . . I admire Aldrich for seeing it through. It's his greatest public success, but not his best film."

He and his bride quickly conspired together to raise Bronson's profile. She talked him into doing projects he never would have done otherwise. Having turned down all three of Italian director Sergio Leone's stylized "spaghetti" westerns, Bronson finally gave in and accepted a role in Leone's epic *Once Upon a Time in the West* (1968). Leone called him "the greatest actor I ever worked with," and the film proved a sensation in international cinema. It was also the only one of Leone's westerns to bomb at the box office in the US, after its American distributor edited the film beyond comprehension.

Undeterred, Bronson continued his European output with Jill Ireland's sage advice. Agreeing to roles Ireland advised him on, Bronson often shared the screen with his wife in such immensely popular thrillers as *Rider on the Rain* (1970), *Cold Sweat* (1970), and *Someone Behind the Door* (1971). The rest of the world's film audiences had discovered through these perfectly tailored vehicles a screen persona to which Bronson's own country remained largely oblivious. What had begun in *The Dirty Dozen* playing Joe Wladislaw carried over into his starring roles: strong, stoic, set with world-weary moral fiber, capable of frightening violence when provoked—and in these films, he was always provoked. He was, in essence, an American samurai, to every country in the world except America. The US caught up when the uncut version of *Once Upon a Time in the West* was released in 1970. The Motion Picture Exhibitors Association would nominate Bronson for Best Supporting Actor. By that time, however, he had been voted the single most popular film star in the world.

Charles Bronson's international popularity in the early 1970s seemed unstoppable; everywhere, that is, except in his native land. He was still working in projects largely financed or directed by Europeans, but the subject matter was becoming more westernized in what seemed an attempt to woo American audiences.

With the Hollywood film industry in free fall and audiences open to more varied styles of filmmaking, studio execs did what they always had in the past: exploit sex and violence. Bronson wouldn't be their go-to guy for sex, but when it came to violence, he was welcomed with open arms. He starred in such international hits as *Red Sun* (1971) with Toshirô Mifune, Alain Delon, and Ursula Andress, and played the title character in the Native American revenge film *Chato's Land* (1972), wearing little more than a loincloth throughout most of the picture. Then came the hugely successful hit man action film *The Mechanic* (1972), followed by the *Godfather* wannabe *The Valachi Papers* (1972). The films were all internationally financed but were set mostly in the US. Audiences were catching on, and when Bronson was asked why he felt he was becoming so popular, he reasoned, "A dozen years ago or so, mine was the kind of face nobody wanted to see in the movies. At least not the good guy's face. But times have changed. I seem to have the right face at the right time."

Despite this major success, some things about the man would not change. Richard Fleischer directed Bronson in the very popular *Mr. Majestyk* (1974) and elicited comparisons to Bronson's *Dirty Dozen* costar Lee Marvin, whom Fleischer directed in *The Spikes Gang* (1974). In a 1999 interview, Fleischer said, "Well, it's quite a contrast. I found [Bronson] a very kind of tight actor. Very inhibited. He plays that kind of role where he doesn't let his emotions show, very stone-faced. Lee is quite the opposite, always disjointed and sloppy. That's the way their acting styles were. They were that way. They're completely different."

Following the vengeful melon farmer he had played in *Mr. Majestyk*, Bronson made the film that would forever brand him an urban vigilante. The controversial film *Death Wish* (1974) spawned a franchise that lasted into the 1980s in which he played architect Paul Kersey, mowing down countless vile criminals, not unlike the convicts seen in *The Dirty Dozen*. Jim Dowdall, the armorer on *The Dirty Dozen*, had become a highly successful stuntman and recalled what it was like to work with Bronson again through the years: "I did indeed work with Bronson in Turkey for three months on *You Can't Win 'Em All* (1970) with Tony Curtis. A dreadful movie, and he was as unpleasant as he had been on *The Dirty Dozen*. I then did *Death Wish 3* [1985] or *Death Wish 4* [1987], can't remember which one. It was shot in England, and he was just as unpleasant. Not a nice man at all."

Other cast members benefited from *The Dirty Dozen*'s success in more unique ways. John Cassavetes, who had been blackballed in the industry prior to begrudgingly agreeing to make the film, came out of it with an Oscar nomination and a renewed career. He chose to bankroll it by creating a new way to navigate his creativity. He would continue to star in mainstream films that were either wildly successful—like *Rosemary's Baby* (1968) for Roman Polanski, with whom he did not get along—or lesser-grade films like the biker movie *Devil's Angels* (1967) or the Italian-made heist film *Machine Gun McCain* (1969).

The money Cassavetes made from such roles was then used to make the kind of personal, independent films Ken Hyman had suggested he do with the money from *The Dirty Dozen*. The results put Cassavetes in the vanguard of the independent film movement in America. The releases of *Faces*, *Husbands* (1970), and *A Woman Under the Influence* (1974), which he wrote, directed, and produced, set the tone for the remainder of his career. He also became one of the few filmmakers who was nominated for Oscars for his films as both writer and director in projects that often costarred his wife, Gena Rowlands, his friends Peter Falk and Ben Gazzara, and, occasionally, Lee Marvin's crony, Bob Phillips.

Jim Brown had been touted for an Oscar for his *Dirty Dozen* performance, which allowed him to star in more leading roles in a genre that eventually became a new 1970s film staple. The term "blaxploitation" would come to mean big-grossing, low-budget films about the African American experience. Prior to starring in such films, Brown appeared in such mainstream hits as *Dark of the Sun* (1968), a South African adventure film in which he was paired with Rod Taylor; *Ice Station Zebra* (1968) in a role meant for a white actor; *The Split* (1968), an all-star caper film reuniting him with Ernest Borgnine and Donald Sutherland; *100 Rifles* (1969), in which he had an interracial love scene with Raquel Welch; *Tick, Tick, Tick* (1970) as a black sheriff in a redneck southern town; and *El Condor* (1970) a spaghetti western with Lee Van Cleef. By the early 1970s, he had become a major box office draw with hits such as *Slaughter* (1972), *Black Gunn* (1972), *Slaughter's Big Rip-Off* (1973), and *Three the Hard Way* (1974). Along with actress Pam Grier, martial artist Jim Kelly, and fellow pro baller Fred "the Hammer" Williamson, they were considered the powerful quartet of blaxploitation. The genre eventually faded in popularity, but Brown continued to act in supporting parts in film and on television, eventually parodying his blaxploitation image hilariously in *I'm Gonna Git You Sucka* (1988).

Although he continued his philanthropic work for African Americans, Brown didn't escape controversy. He was arrested several times for domestic violence incidents, and at the age of fifty-two he announced a return to the NFL when his long-standing rushing record of over twelve thousand yards was about to be breached. He didn't play again, of course, but he did candidly discuss his varied adventures in Spike Lee's well-made documentary *Jim Brown: All-American*. He was also portrayed by actor Aldis Hodge in the award-winning fictional film *One Night in Miami . . .* (2020).

The other main members of the original dozen could still be seen in various films and TV shows. Clint Walker played leads and supporting roles in numerous films and TV shows, even teaming up with Charles Bronson again to play the villain in *The White Buffalo* (1977). He appeared in several successful TV movies, survived a near-death skiing accident, and ultimately retired in the 1990s, save for the occasional Hollywood autograph show.

Telly Savalas also kept working, but his appearance in a powerful TV movie entitled *The Marcus-Nelson Murders* (1973) in which he played a New York detective investigating the false conviction of a Black teenager led to the character's getting his own long-running and very popular TV show, *Kojak*. The show ran from 1973 to 1978 and spawned several TV movies made well into the 1980s.

Following the success of the film, Trini López cowrote and recorded the song "The Ballad of the Dirty Dozen." It was not one of his sixteen top-ten hits in the decade. Other than a few TV appearances playing himself on various shows, he never acted again. His singing career continued successfully in various folk and pop venues until his death at age eighty-three from COVID-19 in 2020.

The remaining major cast members of *The Dirty Dozen* all continued to work in various capacities throughout their lives. The likes of Robert Ryan, Ernest Borgnine, Robert Webber, Richard Jaeckel, and Ralph Meeker were regular, familiar faces in films and episodic television shows and movies from the rest of the 1960s well into the 1980s.

Ryan returned to the stage several times before his passing in 1973. Webber worked steadily through the years, often playing a smarmy white-collar heavy. He was rediscovered by director Blake Edwards and played a poignant gay songwriter in *10* (1979) and was hilarious in the Hollywood satire *S.O.B.* (1981). He passed away in 1989 at the age of sixty-four. Jaeckel also kept working, receiving a well-deserved Oscar nomination for Paul Newman's *Sometimes a Great Notion* (1971). He also was a member of Robert Aldrich's stock company, appearing in two more of the director's films. He, along with

Ernest Borgnine and Telly Savalas, was not yet done with *The Dirty Dozen*. They appeared in several made-for-TV sequels. Ralph Meeker remained an in-demand character actor as well, but he never regained the heights of his popularity in the 1950s and 1960s. He died following a massive heart attack in 1988 at the age of sixty-seven.

Of the remaining bottom six, only Donald Sutherland proved to be a true breakout star. Fellow Canadian Tom Busby (Milo Vladek) worked sporadically as an actor through the years, mostly on the BBC. However, he did have other pursuits, including teaching acting classes for children, becoming a casting agent for films (most notably for John Cassavetes's *Husbands*), and occasionally directing for the BBC. He died of a heart attack in 2003. His daughter, Siân Busby, went on to become a successful novelist before succumbing to lung cancer in 2012.

Upon his return to the US, Al Mancini (Tassos Bravos) taught acting for the next thirty years at the Beverly Hills Playhouse. He continued to act in small roles, most impressively as Gandhi on Steve Allen's innovative historical talk show *Meeting of Minds*. Mancini died in 2007 at the age of seventy-four.

Like some of his costars, Ben Carruthers (Glenn Gilpin) also had a spotty career in both films and music. He had made friends with other Black actors—such as his *Shadows* costar Rupert Crosse, Otis Young, and Louis Gossett Jr.—and worked often in England. His son Caine recalls that when he was six years old, "My mother put *The Dirty Dozen* on TV and I watched with my brother. When my father gets his foot stuck, we both freaked out." According to his son, Ben Carruthers died of spinal cancer in 1983 at the premature age of forty-seven, not liver failure as is often stated as his father's cause of death. Caine became the bass player for the soul/ska band the Untouchables but is currently a professional dog trainer.

The actor who studied Aldrich's work, Stuart Cooper (Roscoe Lever), went on to become a prolific director of film and television. The aforementioned *Overlord* was his creatively imagined retelling of D-Day, shot in black-and-white and ingeniously intercut with actual footage from the invasion. It was heralded as one of the best films of its kind. Cooper has been so active of late that he had to regrettably decline to be interviewed for this book.

Last is Colin Maitland (Seth Sawyer), who gives the final word on *The Dirty Dozen*. The eighty-year-old Britisher is now happily retired from the BBC as a sports reporter and writer but considers his experience in *The Dirty Dozen* an undeniable career highlight. "It is grubby and it is real," he said of the film. "I think that's why it works so well, and why I think the film has continued." As for his role in the film, he said, "I get the feeling that I was actually involved in one of the best movies of its type. It was a groundbreaking movie, and I was there. A very small part of it—I don't kid myself about it in any way. I was there, and I was able to watch . . . some of the finest actors that ever were, actually working, and I was right there next to them. People like Cassavetes and Marvin and these kind of actors. I feel it was an absolute privilege just to be involved."

The film's lead actor, Lee Marvin, and the author of the original novel, E. M. Nathanson, were also inextricably bound to the lasting legacy of *The Dirty Dozen*, which will be explored in the next chapter. The legacy, in many ways, still echoes to this day. That ongoing influence, and its many incarnations, created a cottage industry of sorts that exploded immediately following the film's success.

15

COMBAT FATIGUE VERSUS
ENDURING LEGACY

Since making *The Dirty Dozen* in 1967, the roller coaster ride of successful and unsuccessful films continued across several decades for Lee Marvin. The highs included Sam Fuller's *The Big Red One* (1980) and Michael Apted's *Gorky Park* (1983). The lows were everything from Terence Young's *The Klansman* to Mark Robson's *Avalanche Express* (1979). It all seemed to come to a grinding halt in the early 1980s. He had married Pam Feeley, an old girlfriend from Woodstock, won a grueling palimony suit against Michelle Triola, and, exhausted from the Hollywood lifestyle, had relocated to Tucson, Arizona, in the 1970s.

In the summer of 1984 Marvin's grown son, Christopher, came from California; as he remembers, "I went to visit him, and we're sitting in the kitchen. He had this nice counter in the middle of the kitchen and you could, like, lean against it, eat crackers and sardines, and just talk across the thing. I saw the script and said, 'What's this?' He said, 'Aww, some goddamned sequel to *The Dirty Dozen*. Listen to a line from this. Isn't this shit or what?' I said, 'Yeah, Dad, you don't have to do that shit.' I called him like a month later, and he said, 'I gotta leave.' I said, 'Where you going?' And he said, 'I gotta go do this.' When he told me it was the sequel, I teased him with, 'You asshole!' He said, 'Yeah, shit, I know I told you I wasn't going to do it.' I said, 'Well, enjoy it, man.' I mean, it was just pure hell. He said he needed the kick, man. That's how it works."

And that is indeed how it worked. It took almost twenty years for it to work that way for Marvin, but almost from the moment the original film was released, a never-ending parade of imitations, sequels, out-and-out rip-offs, and, finally, homages began a march through popular media that still shows no sign of stopping. Within three months of the release of the film in June of 1967, the ABC network had a TV series on the air!

The western TV-show craze that began with Clint Walker's *Cheyenne* in the 1950s eventually faded into the spy craze of the 1960s, begun by the popularity of James Bond. It isn't often remembered, but ABC attempted to single-handedly revive the still-popular WWII movie craze with television in the 1960s. It began with *Combat!* (1962–67) and stretched through *12 O'Clock High* (1964–67), *The Rat Patrol* (1966–68), and a combination WWII and spy show in the short-lived *Blue Light* (1966). Coincidentally, during the run of *Combat!*, Telly Savalas, John Cassavetes, Charles Bronson, and Lee Marvin all guest-starred in various episodes.

In the last season of *Combat!*, the most popular of ABC's WWII shows, an unaired episode became the pilot of a new show. Entitled "The Big Con," the episode had characters from *Combat!* interact with a group of soldiers who would be the cast of a spin-off showed called *Garrison's Gorillas*, which started its short run on September 5, 1967. The premise may sound

familiar: the US Army recruits four convicts who are prom-
ised a return to civilian life after the war if they participate
in commando raids. No real stars emerged from the show's
twenty-six-episode run, but a historical footnote did. When
the show aired in reruns in China in the 1980s, it proved so
popular that government meetings were rescheduled so public
officials could watch it.

China may have relished the *Dirty Dozen*–adjacent show,
but Hollywood was still just getting started. A little less than
one year to the day after the release of *The Dirty Dozen*, William Holden starred in an obvious rehash entitled *The Devil's
Brigade* that opened on May 22, 1968. Directed by western
movie veteran Andrew McLaglen and apparently based on a
true story, the film has Holden playing an American colonel
ordered to oversee the recruitment and training of recalcitrant
GI misfits in tandem with a highly professional Canadian unit.
Spit-and-polish Cliff Robertson is in charge of the Canadians,
and a cigar-chomping Vince Edwards is in charge of the GIs.

More than just the premise, the plot itself constantly apes
the *Dirty Dozen* in its brawls, competition, growing respect,
and even the need for a mission to prove the men are capable of
an even bigger mission. Holden looks tired throughout, but the
film does have some watchable moments courtesy of the burly
Claude Akins and *Dozen* veteran Richard Jaeckel.

The critics not only universally panned the film but, coming so close on the heels of *The Dirty Dozen*, wasted no time in
noting the obvious. "An uneven combination of the worst of *The
Dirty Dozen* and the best of *What Price Glory*," wrote "Murf" in
Variety. "The irony here is that the story actually happened, as
opposed to the somewhat fictitious plot of *Dozen*."

Critic Judith Crist, who gave the likes of *The Great Escape*
and *The Dirty Dozen* rave reviews, did not feel the same about

The Devil's Brigade. In *New York* magazine she wrote, "One can, as in the case of *The Dirty Dozen*, even see a logical truth in the proposition that it takes a psychopath to indulge in the psychopathic activity of war with feeling and gusto. Further, the commando-wartime aspect permits us to see human flesh desecrated by more than shot and shell; what marvelous close-ups we can get of garroting, of bashing, of sinking knife and shiv into meat and the freshets of red stuff thereby released!"

Vincent Canby, who had replaced the retired Bosley Crowther at the *New York Times*, also pulled the knives out on *Devil's Brigade*: "There is hardly a character, a situation, or a line of dialogue that has not served a useful purpose in some earlier movie or television show. Now with the passage of time, the characters, the situations, and the lines have begun to look very tired and very empty, like William Holden's eyes."

The critic at *Time* magazine may have summed it up best in predicting what would eventually become a cottage industry: "As a mainstream rough-and-rumble military movie—which is based on actual events—offers few new sights or insights. After nearly three decades of World War II films, it is hardly surprising that Hollywood is beginning to suffer from combat fatigue." Holden would fare infinitely better the following year with the release of *The Wild Bunch*.

Cast members of the original *Dirty Dozen* would occasionally be seen together in similar projects, such as Telly Savalas and Donald Sutherland costarring in the Clint Eastwood vehicle *Kelly's Heroes*, which included the unlikely casting of comedian Don Rickles. A motley group of WWII soldiers gets wind of a hidden cache of Nazi gold and sets out to find it, not to secure their freedom but out of pure greed. Along the way they accidentally become war heroes. The offbeat premise suffers from Eastwood's wooden performance but is quite entertaining thanks largely to Savalas, Sutherland, and the veteran cast of character actors.

Four of the principal participants in *The Dirty Dozen* reunited in 1973 for an equally off-the-beaten path film. Producer Ken Hyman, director Robert Aldrich, and stars Lee Marvin and Ernest Borgnine reteamed for *Emperor of the North*. The Depression-era tale pitted well-heeled hobo A#1 (Marvin) against sadistic conductor Shack (Borgnine) in an all-out war as A#1 bets he can ride Shack's train with annoying novice Cigarette (Keith Carradine), playing both ends against the middle in vying for the film's title. The parable of the individual battling authority with a young upstart muddling the works was lost on most critics, but the film did climax with an amazing fight between Marvin and Borgnine.

"Yeah, I employed him," recalled Hyman about working again with Aldrich. "I originally was going to do it with Sam Peckinpah, but Sam became unavailable. I had limited interest in any of the major (studios') financing, so I had to move quick. So, I went with Aldrich as a second choice."

In working with Marvin after *The Dirty Dozen*, Hyman added, "He was fine. No problem. Lee . . . you know, if you played it straight with Lee, he was no problem. People are all the same. Some quirks and idiosyncrasies. Lee was a boozer, but I could drink with him pretty good. We were friends."

Asked if he considered any projects after the box-office failure of *Emperor*, the ninety-four-year-old Hyman recently said, "Well, I was living in England and I didn't like commuting to Los Angeles or New York. That was that. You know, I was a grown-up, and I said if I find something wonderful that I really want to do, I'll do it, if I'm able to. Being an independent producer, you got to find a relationship and the money before you consider that you're going to make the movie, unless you're

Howard Hughes." Since no project tempted him, he retired to the English countryside with his photographer wife, Caroline, their children, and their grandchildren.

The cliché that imitation is the sincerest form of flattery laid low for a short while. However, the original *Inglorious Bastards* (1978) put a new twist on the overused premise. The film even went so far as to brazenly advertise, "Whatever the Dirty Dozen did, they do it dirtier!" The Italian–made film certainly took its cues from *The Dirty Dozen* in its tale of condemned soldiers being sent to the stockade but given a shot at redemption when their convoy is attacked by Germans on the way to prison.

Five of the convicts manage to escape, including convicted Lt. Robert Yeager (Bo Svenson) and wily Pvt. Canfield (Fred Williamson). They and the others agree to try to make it to Switzerland, despite their ongoing infighting, hurling of racial slurs, and the discovery of a Nazi soldier who's also escaping. The action is almost nonstop as they encounter more Nazis, French partisans, and the American Col. Buckner (Ian Bannen), who recruits them for a mission to blow up a German train carrying the prototype of the V-2 rocket. The combat scenes are impressive and the story is as far-fetched as that of *The Dozen*, but it rivals the original for pure entertainment.

The march of imitation and/or homage, depending on your point of view, continued into the early 1980s. The story goes that one summer afternoon, NBC's president of entertainment Brandon Tartikoff rented the video of *The Dirty Dozen*. Later that evening he went to the movies and saw *The Road Warrior* (1981). The next morning, Tartikoff wrote a note to himself: "There must be a way to combine the two for television." He included the likes of *The Magnificent Seven* and TV's *Mission: Impossible*. His final thought was to add, "The people you go to

do something when no one else can, using off-center characters." Thus *The A-Team* was born.

Running from 1983 to 1987, *The A-Team* starred George
Peppard, Mr. T, Dwight Schultz, and Dirk Benedict as four
soldiers who, wrongly court-martialed, escape to Los Angeles
and try to clear their names while fighting real criminals. Tartikoff hired Stephen J. Cannell and Frank Lupo to write and
produce *The A-Team*. After its run on TV, it later spawned a
theatrical film in 2010 starring Liam Neeson, Bradley Cooper,
Jessica Biel, and Patrick Wilson. A planned sequel was scrapped
when the first film did poorly at the box office. Consequently,
the less said of the show or the film, the better.

Two years after the premiere of *The A-Team* came the first
of three TV-movie sequels to *The Dirty Dozen* to air on NBC.
Despite what he had told his son, Lee Marvin dutifully agreed
to star in *The Dirty Dozen: Next Mission*, so long as it was filmed
in England and not Yugoslavia, as the producers had wanted.
Also reprising their roles were Ernest Borgnine and Richard
Jaeckel. "I can't remember a more bittersweet experience on
a picture," recalled Borgnine. Citing how tired and haggard
Marvin looked, he added, "We did our work, reprised our roles
in this uninspired clambake, and got the hell out of there."

The twenty-five-day shoot went relatively smoothly, with the
new, young dozen vying for screen time. The cast included
the likes of Ken Wahl of *Wiseguy*, Larry Wilcox of *CHiPs*,
and Sonny Landham of *48 Hrs.* (1982), among others. Director Andrew McLaglen didn't change much from the original,
nor did the end product contain any of the film's excitement
with a ridiculous plot to keep Hitler alive. Marvin joked to a
reporter that even though Bronson had survived the original,
"We couldn't get him because he's too busy cleaning up the
alleys of America." Once again, the less said the better.

One thing that didn't change was the general way in which Marvin treated his coworkers, even the day players. Jim Dowdall, the young armorer from the original film, had become a stuntman and worked briefly on the film. "I turned a motorbike and sidecar over," he recalled. "I just came in to do two or three days, and that was one of a part of a chase sequence. . . . I flipped the thing over and that was it, thanks, go home and good night. But [Lee Marvin] was there.

"This is twenty years later and it's in the winter, and we're all cold and all. I now have a German uniform and helmet. I'm going into the dining bus to eat my breakfast. I can feel somebody's eyes on me. I look down to the end of the dining bus and there's Marvin, and he looks at me. He does that thing as though he was cocking a gun, as he did twenty-plus years ago. He points his finger and says, 'It's you, isn't it?' I never felt so . . . I felt ten feet tall at that point, that he should recognize me. It was twenty years later, and I was in a completely different department in those days. . . . I had great respect for him. He was a top man, as far as I'm concerned."

Also not involved in the sequel was the original director, who'd had several hits and misses over the years. To his credit, Robert Aldrich once again struck motion picture pay dirt in a film similar in content to *The Dirty Dozen*. Leonard Maltin called *The Longest Yard* (1974) "an audience picture if there ever was one; hilarious, bone-crunching comedy!" Burt Reynolds played an incarcerated quarterback who organizes and plays in a football game featuring guards against prisoners. In typical Aldrich fashion, the guards and warden are more tyrannical and corrupt than the prisoners. It all comes to a rousing finish nonetheless. The film was later revamped with Adam Sandler in a practically scene-for-scene remake in 2005.

Aldrich indeed managed to keep working for almost a full

decade despite ongoing health problems. He also served two terms as president of the Directors Guild of America, winning unprecedented benefits for its membership. From 1975 to 1983 he directed five more films, none of them clicking with critics or audiences despite the quality of *Twilight's Last Gleaming* (1977) and *The Choirboys* (1977). His health continued to deteriorate to the point that when Lee Marvin visited him in the hospital and asked if he needed anything, the old veteran of more than forty years of filmmaking told him, "Yeah, a better script." Aldrich died on December 5, 1983, at the age of sixty-five.

Lee Marvin didn't live much longer. Following several complications resulting from his years of drinking and five-pack-a-day cigarette habit, he succumbed to a heart attack in the hospital at the age of sixty-three on August 29, 1987. Like Aldrich, whom he worked with three times, Marvin left behind a legacy of great films that are still being appreciated, even by younger audiences, to this day. He was buried with full military honors at Arlington National Cemetery.

As the decade of the 1980s wore on, so too did the *Dirty Dozen* franchise. Two more sequels were aired, both starring Telly Savalas: *The Dirty Dozen: The Deadly Mission* (1987) and *The Dirty Dozen: The Fatal Mission* (1988). The first costarred Larry Wilcox, while the second had Erik Estrada, lead characters Jon and Ponch from TV's popular cop show *CHiPs*. In both TV movies Savalas played a new character named Maj. Wright, commanding new sets of dozens on improbable missions as ordered, as always, by Ernest Borgnine. What the makers of all these incarnations failed to take into account was the emphasis the original film placed on character, not necessarily the mission. The characters in the rehashes were more like caricatures than real people. As for Telly "the Golden Greek" Savalas, he lived well off the success of *Kojak* and its several TV-movie sequels, and, surrounded by his family, passed away at the age of seventy-two in 1994.

As if the badly made TV movies weren't enough, the then new Fox network attempted a *Dirty Dozen* TV series in 1988 starring Ben Murphy as group leader Lt. Danko. Set before the original in 1943, the series was kicked off with a two-hour premiere episode. "The television series was awful," said author Mick Nathanson. He added with a laugh, "I think it was shot in a telephone booth in Dubrovnik." The producers had actually contacted Nathanson to possibly write an episode. "They sent it over to Fox for approval, and Fox shot it down," said Nathanson. "They thought it was too gritty, too real. They wanted characters who were slick, with-it eighties characters." The producers' concept of the show having hip, slick characters meant that they shot thirteen episodes and aired only seven, canceling the show for its poor ratings.

Since the publication of the original novel in 1965, Nathanson had not, of course, been resting on his royalties. He continued to write other novels, such as *The Latecomers* (1970), and cowrote a nonfiction true-crime novel with the person who perpetrated the crime, Louise Thoresen. Nathanson described it as "the story of a woman's life with her no-good husband, and she wound up killing him. Loves him, but kills him." Titled *It Gave Everybody Something to Do* (1973), there was talk of a film version that would star Jill Clayburgh and be directed by Mike Nichols, but it never came to pass. Nathanson also cowrote *Knight's Cross* (1993) with Col. Aaron Bank, who, like the fictional John Reisman, was in the OSS during WWII and later was the founder of the Special Forces unit known as the Green Berets. Nathanson also wrote *Lovers and Schemers* (2003), a tale of love and suspense in Orange County, California, that stretches from the 1960s to the 1990s.

John Reisman was not, however, in Nathanson's thoughts for his bestselling 1987 novel. "I wanted nothing more to do with John Reisman and the Dirty Dozen," he told the *Los Angeles Times* in that same year. Once he began writing the book, he decided, "as I wrote it, it was the same guy. Then it hit me: Why not? There was no good reason why it shouldn't be the same guy."

The work was titled *A Dirty Distant War: The Sequel to the Dirty Dozen* and published by Viking. Nathanson said of it in 2008, "John Reisman, about three or four months after *The Dirty Dozen* mission ends, goes to Asia to Burma, China, [and] French Indochina, which later became Vietnam. He has extraordinary adventures, including [meeting] Ho Chi Minh."

Asked if it explains what became of the dozen, he added, "Yes, it's explained early in *A Dirty Distant War*, not in the first chapter but soon after. He does bring some of the men [Bowren, Wladislaw, and Sawyer] to Asia, after he's there. He goes on a very singular mission. There comes a time when he can use their help. He sends for the guys who survived the mission in Europe. That's how we learn what happened to each. I don't even remember which ones. They serve a minor role in *A Dirty Distant War*, which is a novel mainly about Reisman and what he does. It's filled with the international politics of the day. What happens in that novel reflects what happens a generation later in our war in Vietnam. It's from August '44 to March '46 when this story takes place. It ends with WWII still going on, but you can see the ending coming."

The sequel sold well and was well received by most critics. Nathanson's good friend and fellow author Frank McAdams recently said, "Mick made an attempt to get the sequel to *The Dirty Dozen* [made] as a film, with Hyman as producer. Sadly, *A Dirty Distant War* never made it to the screen. As I noted, I felt that *Dirty Distant War* was better than *The Dirty Dozen*. I told that to Mick once. He smiled and nodded. When I finished the manuscript of *Dirty Distant War*, I sat on my couch in the living room, staring at the last paragraph. I didn't move for several minutes."

Nathanson had planned a revamped version of *The Dirty Dozen* he would self-publish through his own company, Regenesis Press, when major publishers passed on it. The basic plot remained the same, but he cleaned up what he considered could have been better written. "I found things I could polish easily," he said at the time. "Some lines that I thought could be better. None of the characters or plot. It's the same, but it's polished in about thirty or forty places." To date, it has yet to see the light of day. Nathanson passed away in 2016 of heart failure at the age of eighty-eight.

Director Joe Dante, known for the popular 1984 film *Gremlins* and a true purveyor of Baby Boomer pop culture, directed the 1998 film *Small Soldiers*. The fantasy plot involved action figure dolls doing battle with their more peace-loving counterparts. The lead action figure, named Chip Hazard, bore more than a passing resemblance to Lee Marvin. Lending his voice to the character was Tommy Lee Jones, an actor whose resemblance to Marvin is more than coincidental. For good measure, Dante hired the likes of Ernest Borgnine, Jim Brown, Clint Walker, and George Kennedy to provide the voices of some of the other action figures. "They were using us for name value. They were getting everybody they could from *The Dirty Dozen*," Walker said. "I think everybody enjoyed seeing everybody. It was good. I enjoyed seeing the fellas. I think the toy soldiers were a great deal."

In the original 1967 classic, Trini López made an abrupt exit from the film after demanding more money from Aldrich, so it's rather ironic that when *Small Soldiers* went into production, as Clint Walker recounted, "Trini López was there, but again, I guess they couldn't make the deal. He never did anything, so I don't know."

It would prove to be the last hurrah for several of the original dozen. Richard Jaeckel was not available, as he passed away from cancer at the age of seventy at the Motion Picture and Television Fund retirement home in Woodland Hills, California, a year before the film was made. George Kennedy died on February 28, 2016, just ten days after his ninety-first birthday. Borgnine passed in 2012 at the age of ninety-five, and Walker passed in 2018 at the age of ninety.

Before his passing, Walker discovered something other than his career to be proud of. His daughter, Valerie, was among the first female pilots hired by Western Airlines (which merged with Delta in the 1980s) and was the first female pilot at that airline to reach the rank of first officer. According to Valerie, her father never wanted her to fly. She said, "However, a few years ago, before he died, he was inducted into the Cowboy Hall of Fame. I went there to support him. They had a big TV or a monitor where they'd play all of the actors, photos, and scenes, and do a rundown of their life. Somebody had asked Dad, 'What are you most proud of?' And he threw a picture of me up there in my airline uniform. And he says, 'I'm most proud of my daughter, and what she's accomplished with her life.' I just broke down in tears. It meant so much to me. Before Dad died, we became very close, and [I] feel very blessed."

The last major player of the original *Dirty Dozen* cast, Charles Bronson, continued his output of urban violence films, with only a few turns toward better material. *Hard Times* (1975) and a few others were the exceptions, as critics took most of his films to task while his audiences continued to show up. "I don't make movies for critics," he said. "They don't pay anyhow."

In 1987 he made another programmer entitled *Assassination*, which proved to be a bittersweet experience for the actor. It would be the last time he would appear onscreen with his wife and most frequent costar, Jill Ireland. Ireland had survived a very public bout with breast cancer, as well as the overdose of her adopted son, Jason McCallum, all of which she wrote about in two bestselling memoirs. Sadly, the cancer returned, and on May 18, 1990, Ireland succumbed to it. The very private Bronson was forced to admit, "One of the difficult parts of being a public person married to someone who was seriously ill is that people asked, 'So, how's your wife?' I found it difficult. They were strangers." A TV movie about their lives that Bronson tried to keep from the airwaves was broadcast with Jill Clayburgh as Ireland and Lance Henriksen as Bronson.

Bronson himself had ventured into the realm of TV movies with the HBO drama *Act of Vengeance* (1986), playing real-life United Mine Workers union president Jock Yablonski. He gave one of his best performances in this now largely forgotten early cable project, even going so far as to shave his mustache for the first time since *Hard Times*.

As for his final years, it would be comforting to say that after a string of cheaply made *Death Wish* sequels, Bronson's last screen appearance was in actor Sean Penn's directorial debut, *The Indian Runner* (1991). Bronson had a small role, also sans mustache, as the father of the two lead characters. He had a telephone scene in which his last words were "Good night, son" before he commits suicide. It would have been a poignant cinematic epitaph for the actor—one for which he received a standing ovation when the film was shown at the Cannes Film Festival. Instead, he made *Death Wish V: The Face of Death* (1994). He had also made a semi-return to television in a series of forgettable TV movies playing the patriarch to a *Family of Cops* (1995–1999). In the films was a young actress named Kim Weeks, who would become the third and final Mrs. Bronson in 1998.

Following hip replacement surgery the same year, Bronson retired from acting and remained secluded, and it was reported that he had developed Alzheimer's disease. A bout of pneumonia officially ended his life on August 30, 2003, at the age of eighty-one. A legal battle over his estate ensued among surviving family members, with the public left to inherit the legacy of his films, both good and bad.

One of the more appropriate tributes to *The Dirty Dozen* was its release on home video. When Warner Bros. bought the rights to the film, it released an impressive volume on VHS, followed by a two-DVD set with all the bells and whistles. Included with the film is running commentary by surviving cast members, author Nathanson, and military expert Capt. Dale Dye. Also included are such extras as the first sequel, the theatrical trailer, an introduction by Ernest Borgnine, and a period documentary made on location. Two more recently made documentaries are also part of the set, as is the Marine training film *Marine Corps Combat Leadership Skills* (1986), hosted and narrated by Lee Marvin. It would be his last onscreen appearance.

The current crop of filmmakers who have grown up seeing *The Dirty Dozen* on TV or, like Ron Howard, viewed it in theaters in their youth have taken the enduring legacy of the film to new heights. Writer and director Quentin Tarantino bought the rights to *Inglorious Bastards* to make his own version with no connection to the original, changing the title to *Inglourious Basterds* (2009). Instead of convicts, the protagonists are Jewish refugees led by redneck Lt. Aldo Raine (Brad Pitt) who team up to fight and defeat the Nazis. To provide a fitting homage to *The Dirty Dozen*, Tarantino created a climactic scene in which high-ranking officials of the Third Reich, including Hitler, were incinerated—rather fittingly, in a movie theater.

Director James Gunn is so enamored with *The Dirty Dozen* that primary elements of it have appeared in his most successful films, including *Guardians of the Galaxy* (2014), *The Suicide Squad* (2021), and their subsequent sequels. Most impressive of all, in 2019 it was announced in the media that director David Ayer would write and direct a *Dirty Dozen* remake. The concept had been shelved for a while, but it has been revived again as recently as May 2022.

In 2001, the American Film Institute named *The Dirty Dozen* one of the one hundred most thrilling films of all time. The bottom line is, *The Dirty Dozen* will certainly survive both time and cultural change. When all is said and done, the film's enduring legacy wins over combat fatigue every time.

ACKNOWLEDGMENTS

After twenty years of research, the publication of *Lee Marvin: Point Blank* changed my life. I have no one to thank more for that minor miracle than my agent, Mike Hamilburg. Mike passed away in 2016, leaving me basically in free fall. Enter Lee Sobel. In a miraculously short time, I signed with him and got a contract to write this book with Kensington Press. Luckily my editor at Kensington, Gary Goldstein, is a big *Dirty Dozen* fan, which helped immensely. To them both, I humbly express my deepest gratitude.

When I mentioned this project to fellow author and biographer Beverly Gray in its earliest stages, she volunteered an unpublished interview she had conducted with author E. M. Nathanson a few years before he passed. This amazingly generous act of kindness made this book possible.

Several of the photos in this book were graciously contributed by the interview subjects I spoke to. For a full list of those individuals, please see the bibliography. To all those past and present who took the time to talk with me, whether in person, by phone, or by e-mail, I thank you. Help in getting the interviews and in pointing me in the right direction was provided by Catherine Olim, David Weston, Caroline Hyman, Tom Fordy, Deb Elsie, Nat Segaloff, Frank McAdams, Alain Silver, Graham White, Steve Rubin, Mike Perry, Robbie McGuire and Matt Moss of Fighting on Film fame, Paul Woodage, and Steve Saragossi.

Probably *the* greatest source for any film historian, researcher, or film enthusiast is the Margaret Herrick Library at the Academy of Motion Picture Arts and Sciences. I am extremely grateful to all those involved in making my time there so worthy. They include Larry Karaszewski, Matt Severs, Genevieve Maxwell, and Louise Hilton. I thank you all. Lest I forget, thank you to the good folks at the Long Beach Public Library. One should never forget the treasures to be discovered at one's local library.

On a personal note, I would be remiss if I didn't include the people I know who have encouraged me and this work: Mike Barrow, Sacha Bennett, Julie Schneider Buchanan, Joshua Curtis, Larry Deutchman, Tiffany Driscoll, Harriette Ellis, David Hogan, Jeff Mantor, Shawn Marengo, Sean Murphy, Mike Phillips, Chen Pollin, Tim Schaffner, Dan and Vickie Silverman, Marcus Williams, and Nick Zagone.

Special and separate thanks must go to my family for their moral support. Sisters Belinda Becerra and Fern Epstein, nieces Natalie Stasiewicz and Danielle Becerra and their husbands Matt Stasiewicz and Garett Gruessing, I thank you all. If there's anyone I haven't mentioned, it's a result of failing memory, not a lack of gratitude.

I've purposely saved the best for last. Girl Friday, Editor Supreme, Bringer of the Bacon, and the single greatest cheerleader the world has ever known, I love you to the moon and back, Barbara.

BIBLIOGRAPHY

BOOKS

Arnold, Edwin T., and Eugene L. Miller. *The Films and Career of Robert Aldrich*. Knoxville: University of Tennessee Press, 1986.

———. *Robert Aldrich: Interviews*. Jackson: University of Mississippi Press, 2004.

Biskind, Peter. *Easy Riders, Raging Bulls: How the Sex-Drugs-and-Rock 'n' Roll Generation Saved Hollywood*. New York: Touchstone Books, 1998.

Bogdanovich, Peter. *Who the Devil Made It: Conversations with Legendary Film Directors*. New York: Ballantine Books, 1997.

———. *Who the Hell's In It: Conversations with Hollywood's Legendary Actors*. New York: Ballantine Books, 2004.

Borgnine, Ernest. *Ernie: The Autobiography*. New York: Citadel Press, 2008.

Boorman, John. *Adventures of a Suburban Boy*. London: Faber & Faber, 2003.

Brode, Douglas. *The Films of the Sixties: From La Dolce Vita to Easy Rider*. New York: Citadel Press, 1980.

Brokaw, Tom. *The Greatest Generation*. New York: Random House, 1998.

Bronson, Harriett. *Charlie & Me: A Memoir*. Woodland Hills, CA: Timberlake Press, 2011.

Brown, Jim, and Steve Delsohn. *Out of Bounds*. New York: Zebra Books, 1989.

Callan, Michael Feeney. *Sean Connery*. New York: Stein & Day, 1985.

Carney, Ray, and John Cassavetes. *Cassavetes on Cassavetes*. London: Faber & Faber, 2001.

Cassavetes, John. *Faces*. New York: Signet, 1970.

Charity, Tom. *John Cassavetes: Lifeworks*. London: Omnibus Press, 2001.

Corman, Roger, with Jim Jerome. *How I Made a Hundred Movies in Hollywood and Never Lost a Dime*. New York: Random House, 1990.

Davis, Bette, and Whitney Stine. *Mother Goddam*. New York: Berkeley, 1974.

Downing, David. *Charles Bronson*. New York: St. Martin's Press, 1983.

Epstein, Dwayne. *Lee Marvin: Point Blank*. Tucson, AZ: Schaffner Press, 2013.

Fine, Marshall. *Accidental Genius: How John Cassavetes Invented the American Independent Film*. New York: Hyperion, 2005.

Finler, Joel W. *The Movie Directors Story*. London: Octopus Books, Ltd., 1985.

Froug, William. *The Screenwriter Looks at the Screenwriter*. New York: Macmillan, 1972.

Gray, Beverly. *Seduced by Mrs. Robinson: How The Graduate Became the Touchstone of a Generation*. Chapel Hill, NC: Algonquin Books, 2017.

Hamilton, Ian. *Writers in Hollywood, 1915–1951*. New York: Harper & Row, 1990.

Harbinson, W. A. *Bronson!: A Biographical Portrait*. New York: Pinnacle Books, 1975.

Ireland, Jill. *Life Wish*. Boston: Little, Brown & Co., 1987.

———. *Life Lines*. New York: Warner Books, 1989.

Jacobs, Diane. *Hollywood Renaissance: The New Generation of Filmmakers and Their Works*. New York: Dell Publishing, 1980.

Johnson, Dorris, and Ellen Leventhal, eds. *The Letters of Nunnally Johnson*. New York: Knopf, 1981.

Johnson, Nora. *Flashback: Nora Johnson on Nunnally Johnson*. New York: Doubleday, 1979.

Jones, J. R. *The Lives of Robert Ryan*. Middletown, CT: Wesleyan University Press, 2015.

Kennedy, George. *Trust Me: A Memoir*. Madison, WI: Applause, 2011.

Knopf, Christopher. *Will the Real Me Please Stand Up*. Albany, GA: BearManor Media, 2010.

Krohn, Bill, ed. *Serious Pleasures*. Arles, France: Actes Sud, 1997.

Lentz, Robert J. *Lee Marvin: His Films and Career*. Jefferson, NC: McFarland & Company, 2000.

McAdams, Frank J. *The American War Film: History and Hollywood*. Los Angeles: Figueroa Press, 2005.

McDonough, Jimmy. *Big Bosoms and Square Jaws: The Biography of Russ Meyer, King of the Sex Film*. New York: Crown, 2005.

Maltin, Leonard. *Leonard Maltin's Movie and Video Guide*. New York: Plume, 1989.

Marvin, Betty. *Tales of a Hollywood Housewife: A Memoir by the First Mrs. Lee Marvin*. Bloomington, IN: iUniverse, 2009.

Marvin, Pamela. *Lee: A Romance.* London: Faber & Faber, 1997.

Mordden, Ethan. *Medium Cool: The Movies of the 1960s.* New York: Alfred A. Knopf, 1990.

Naha, Ed. *The Films of Roger Corman: Brilliance on a Budget.* New York: Arco Publishing, 1982.

Nathanson, E. M. *The Dirty Dozen.* New York: Dell, 1965.

———. *A Dirty Distant War: The Sequel to The Dirty Dozen.* New York: Viking, 1987.

Nickens, Christopher. *Bette Davis: A Biography in Photographs.* New York: Doubleday, 1985.

Osborne, Robert. *50 Golden Years of Oscar: The Official History of the Academy of Motion Picture Arts & Sciences.* California: ESE Publishing, 1979.

Obst, Lynda Rosen, ed. *The Sixties.* New York: Rolling Stone Press, 1977.

Passingham, Kenneth. *Sean Connery: A Biography.* New York: St. Martin's Press, 1983.

Peary, Danny, ed. *Close-Ups: The Movie Star Book.* New York: Workman Publishing, 1978.

Pfeiffer, Lee, and Philip Lisa. *The Films of Sean Connery.* New York: Kensington Press, 2001.

Pitts, Michael R. *Charles Bronson: The 95 Films and the 156 Television Appearances.* Jefferson, NC: McFarland & Company, 1999.

Quinlan, David. *Quinlan's Illustrated Directory of Film Stars.* New York: Hippocrene Books, 1981.

———. *Quinlan's Illustrated Guide to Film Directors.* London: Batsford Books, 1983.

Reisser, Dora. *Dora's Story.* Market Harborough, UK: Troubador Publishing, 2016.

Rose, Thomas, ed. *Violence in America: A Historical and Contemporary Reader.* New York: Random House, 1969.

Rubin, Steven Jay. *The Twilight Zone Encyclopedia.* Chicago: Chicago Review Press, 2018.

Shipman, David. *The Great Movie Stars: The International Years.* New York: Hill and Wang, 1972.

Silver, Alain. *Robert Aldrich: A Guide to References and Resources.* Boston: G. K. Hall & Co, 1979.

Silver, Alain, and James Ursini. *What Ever Happened to Robert Aldrich?: His Life and His Films.* New York: Limelight Editions, 1995.

Stempel, Tom. *Screenwriter Nunnally Johnson.* San Diego: A. S. Barnes, 1980.

Symmons, Tom. *The Historical Film in the Era of New Hollywood, 1967–1980.* London: University of London Press, 2016.

Talbot, Paul. *Bronson's Loose Again!: On the Set with Charles Bronson.* Albany, GA: BearManor Media, 2016.

Thomson, David. *The New Biographical Dictionary of Film.* New York: Alfred A. Knopf, 2010.

Travers, Peter, ed. *The Rolling Stone Film Reader.* New York: Pocket Books, 1996.

Vermilye, Jerry. *The Films of Charles Bronson.* New York: Citadel Press, 1980.

Weddle, David. *"If They Move . . . Kill 'Em!": The Life and Times of Sam Peckinpah.* New York: Grove Press, 1994.

Wiley, Mason, and Damien Bona. *Inside Oscar: The Unofficial History of the Academy Awards.* New York: Ballantine Books, 1987.

Williams, Tony. *Body and Soul: The Cinematic Vision of Robert Aldrich.* Lanham, MD: Scarecrow Press, 2004.

Winner, Michael. *Winner Takes All: A Life of Sorts*. London: Robson Books, 2004.

Wise, James E. Jr., and Anne Collier Rehill. *Stars in the Corps: Movie Actors in the United States Marines*. Annapolis, MD: Naval Institute Press, 1999.

Whitney, Steven. *Charles Bronson: Superstar*. New York: Dell, 1975.

Zec, Donald. *Marvin: The Story of Lee Marvin*. New York: St. Martin's Press, 1980.

PERIODICALS

Aldrich, Robert. "You Can't Hang Up the Meat Hook." *New York Herald Tribune*, February 20, 1955.

———. "Director's Formula for a Happy Cast." *Los Angeles Times*, February 6, 1966.

Anon. *Fragile Fox* (aka *Attack!*) production notes. United Artists, 1956.

Anon. *Attack!* pressbook. United Artists, 1956.

Anon. "Miss Godman Bride of Kenneth Hyman." *New York Times*, December 6, 1964.

Anon. "Palance Refuses to Play 'Dirty' Role for Metro." *Daily Variety*, February 22, 1966.

Anon. "Publicity Campaign Announcement." *Lion Power*, April 19, 1967.

Anon. "Tidy Village Claims Foul on Film Team." *Los Angeles Times*, May 23, 1966.

Anon. *The Dirty Dozen* pressbook. MGM, 1966.

Anon. "Chateau Built, Blown Up." *Los Angeles Herald-Examiner*, June 3, 1967.

Anon. "Candid Hollywood." *New Bedford Standard Times*, June 5, 1966.

Anon. "A Private Affair." *Time*, June 30, 1967.

Anon. *"Dirty Dozen* Breaking Dozens of Records." *Citizen-News*, July 5, 1967.

Anon. *"Waves, Born Losers, Dirty Dozen*, All Draw Frowns from Catholics." *Weekly Variety*, July 5, 1967.

Anon. "The Current Cinema: Glory!" *New Yorker*, July 22, 1967.

Anon. "Father and Son." *Cue*, August 5, 1967.

Anon. *"Dirty Dozen* Cleaning Up." *Daily Variety*, August 8, 1967.

Anon. *"Dirty Dozen*: Obscene." *Canyon Crier*, August 24, 1967.

Anon. "Lee the Marvel." *Stage & Cinema*, September 8, 1967.

Anon. *"The Dirty Dozen."* *Esquire*, October 1967.

Anon. "North Pole Express." Emperor of the North Pressbook, 1972.

Anon. "Lee Marvin's Intimate Love Letters to His Mistress Are Revealed for the First Time." *The Star*, March 13, 1979.

Anon. *"The Dirty Dozen* Revived in TV Movie." *Canadian Press*, February 1985.

Anon. "Close-Up: *The Dirty Dozen: Next Mission."* *TV Guide*, February 4, 1985.

Anon. *"The Dirty Dozen*: Rewind." *TNT Monthly Guide*, 2014.

Anon. "Frederick Hyman Obituary." *New York Times*, October 10, 2021.

Bedell, Sally. "How TV Hit *The A Team* Was Born." *New York Times*, April 28, 1983.

Benson, Walter. "Success Came Too Late, Says Lee Marvin." *National Enquirer*, May 15, 1966.

Blumenthal, Ralph. "Richard Jaeckel Is Dead at 70; A

Durable Movie Tough Guy." *New York Times*, June 17, 1997.

Bush, Thomas W. "MGM Earnings, Revenues for Third Quarter Increases Sharply." *Los Angeles Times*, July 14, 1967.

Childers, Thomas. "Readjusting to Postwar Society: Troubled Homecoming." *VFW Magazine*, April 2009.

Connolly, Mike. "Rambling Reporter." *Hollywood Reporter*, May 1966.

———. "Lee Marvin: Some Tough Guy." *Modern Screen*, June 1966.

Crowther, Bosley. "Screen: Brutal Tale of 12 Angry Men." *New York Times*, June 20, 1967.

Daley, Arthur. "Don't Push Me." *New York Times*, August 24, 1966.

Dent, Alan. "Cinema." *Illustrated London News*, August 26, 1967.

Dolgoff, Stephanie. "*The Dirty Dozen*: A 1967 Combat Film Takes Vietnam to World War II." *Cable Guide*, November 1990.

Durgnat, Raymond. "*The Dirty Dozen*: Raymond Durgnat Sees Robert Aldrich's View of Human Nature." *Films & Filming*, October 1967.

Eyles, Allen. "The Private War of Robert Aldrich." *Films & Filming*, September 1967.

Hathaway, Maggie. "'I'm Ready to Quit Football'—Jim Brown." *Los Angeles Sentinel*, January 20, 1966.

Herbstman, Mandel. "REVIEW OF NEW FILM." *Film Daily*, June 16, 1967.

Honeycutt, Kirk. "Maverick Marvin." *Daily News*, February 11, 1986.

Gertner, Richard. "Reviews . . . *The Dirty Dozen.*" *Motion Picture Herald*, June 21, 1967.

Graham, Sheilah. "Lee Marvin Talks Marriage." *New York World-Telegram and Sun*, March 15, 1966.

Greenberg, Abe. "*Dirty Dozen* One of Finest." *Citizen-News*, June 29, 1967.

Gross, Milton. "Jimmy Brown—On Camera." *New York Post*, May 31, 1966.

Jackson, George H. "Gala Event for *Dirty Dozen.*" *Los Angeles Herald-Examiner*, June 20, 1967.

———. "*Dirty Dozen*—A Thriller." *Los Angeles Herald-Examiner*, June 29, 1967.

Knight, Arthur. "Games Martial and Marital." *Saturday Review*, June 27, 1967.

Latte, John. "Lee Marvin Was a Plumber's Apprentice & Dug Septic Tanks." *National Enquirer*, May 7, 1985.

Lewis, Andy, and Mike Barnes. "E. M. Nathanson, *The Dirty Dozen* Author, Dies at 87." *Los Angeles Times*, April 6, 2016.

Liebenson, Donald. "These World War II Heroes Were Dirtier by the *Dozen.*" *Los Angeles Times*, May 19, 2000.

Lowry, Ed. "*The Dirty Dozen*: Program Notes." *Cinema Texas*, Fall 1982.

McCombie, Brian. "Warriors on the Silver Screen." *VFW Magazine*, February 1997.

McLellean, Dennis. "*Dirty Dozen* Author Hawks a Sequel of Betrayal." *Los Angeles Times*, November 28, 1987.

Mahoney, John. "*Dirty Dozen* Should Be One of MGM's Biggest Moneymakers." *Variety*, June 16, 1967.

Manners, Dorothy. "Lee Marvin's Romance a Question Mark." *Los Angeles Herald-Examiner*, August 20, 1966.

Martin, Betty. "Marvin Signed for *Dozen*." *Los Angeles Times*, April 4, 1966.

Melton, William R. "Books and Authors: A Convert to the Hard Sell." *Los Angeles Times*, March 13, 1966.

Muir, Florabel. "A Frank Fellow." *Daily News*, March 11, 1966.

Muller, Kurt. "The Love That's Made David Laugh Again." *Modern Screen*, April 1967.

Murf. "*The Dirty Dozen*." *Variety*, June 21, 1967.

O'Connor, John J. "Television: And Once Again It's *The Dirty Dozen*, as a Series." *New York Times*, April 30, 1988.

O'Sullivan, Katie. "Lee Marvin: 'My Wife Didn't Understand Me.'" *TV and MOVIE SCREEN*, July 1967.

Reisfeld, Bert. "*Dirty Dozen* Study of Wartime Morality." *Los Angeles Times*, September 11, 1966.

Roberts, Tom. "Lee Marvin: 'I Love My Kids, But Oh, You Baby!'" *Movie Mirror*, December 1966.

Ryan, Tim. "*The Dirty Dozen* DVD Release." *Worldly Remains #5*, Spring 2002.

Schickel, Richard. "Harsh Moral from a Grisly Film," *Life*, July 21, 1967.

Schreiberg, Stu. "Lee Marvin: Master of the Uphill Battle." *USA Today*, February 4, 1985.

Scott, John L. "MGM Schedules *Dirty Dozen*." *Los Angeles Times*, May 31, 1963.

Scullen, George. "*The Dirty Dozen*." *Screen Stories*, December 1967.

Silverstone, Lou, and Mort Drucker. "Dirtier by the Dozen." *MAD Magazine*, January 1968.

Steen, Al. "Picture of the Month: *The Dirty Dozen*." *Greater Amusements*, July 1967.

Taylor, Norman. "*The Dirty Dozen.*" *ABC Film Review*, November 1967.

Thomas, Bob. "A Little Respect for Lee Marvin." Associated Press, May 17, 1966.

Thomas, Kevin. "*Dirty Dozen* at Paramount." *Los Angeles Times*, June 25, 1967.

Wall, James M. "Films in Review." *Christian Advocate*, August 24, 1967.

Wallace, William, N. "Jim Brown Uncertain about Pro Football Career." *New York Times*, May 29, 1966.

Weiller, A. H. "Teamwork on the Seine." *New York Times*, January 21, 1965.

Wilson, Earl. "It Happened Last Night: A Bit of Bogart." *New York Post*, April 25, 1966.

Zimmerman, Paul D. "Felony Squad." *Newsweek*, July 3, 1967.

ONLINE SOURCES

Academy of Motion Pictures Arts & Sciences

American Film Institute Catalog

IMDb.com

Coats, Michael. "*The Dirty Dozen*: The 70mm Engagements." in70mm.com, December 2, 2017.

Collis, Chris. "Empire Essay: *The Dirty Dozen* Review." Empire Online, January 1, 2001.

Fordy, Tom. "'Morbid and Disgusting Beyond Words' How *The Dirty Dozen* Blew Up the War Movie Rulebook." *Daily Telegraph*, August 10, 2021.

Johnson, Nunnally, and Lukas Heller. "*The Dirty Dozen* Script." Google Docs, 1966.

Pelan, Tim. "Slaughterhouse Twelve: Robert Aldrich's *The Dirty Dozen.*" Cinephilia & Beyond, 2022.

Seitz, Matt Zoller. "60 Minutes on: *The Dirty Dozen*." Roger Ebert.com, October 2, 2016.

Slifkin, Irv. "All About Aldrich." MovieFanFare.com, October 3, 2012.

Smith, Patrick. "Mercenary Group Head Known as 'Putin's Chef' Filmed Recruiting in Russian Prison." NBCNews. com, September 16, 2022.

Stempel, Tom. "Recollections of Nunnally Johnson Oral History Transcript." Oral History Program, Bancroft Library, UCLA, 1969.

Susman, Gary. "*The Dirty Dozen*: How the Combat Classic Created the Modern Action Film." Moviefone.com, June 15, 2012.

Wikipedia

YouTube

PODCASTS

Fighting on Film

WW2TV

VIDEOS

The Dirty Dozen 2-Disc Special Edition DVD, Warner Video, 2006.

Director's Cut: Jim Brown: All American DVD, Spike Lee, HBO Video, 2003.

Kiss Me Deadly DVD, Robert Aldrich, Criterion, 2011.

INTERVIEWS

Eddie Albert, April 24, 1997, and December 11, 1997

John Andrie, May 22, 2016

Joseph Biroc, October 25, 1994

Caine Carruthers, June 22, 2022

Charles Champlin, October 8, 1994

Roger Corman, December 10, 2015

Suzie Dotan, March 1, 2016 (and e-mail)

Jim Dowdall (e-mail), July 6–8, 2022

Tony Epper, October 29, 1994

Richard Fleischer, May 5, 1999

Guy Galosi, July 25, 2016

Fr. James Hoge, OSB, May 5, 1998

Kenneth Hyman, November 12, 2021, and March 21, 2022

Adam Klugman, November 18, 2015

David Klugman, October 30, 2015

Stanley Kramer, July 4, 1994

Frank McAdams (e-mail), February 5–April 7, 2022

Colin Maitland (e-mail), February 16–March 23, 2022

Betty Marvin, February 12–15, 1995

Christopher Marvin, March 5, 1995

Robert Marvin, June 8, 1996

Meyer Mishkin, July 23, 1994

E. M. Nathanson (unpublished interview by Beverly Gray),
    March 14, 2008

Michael Nathanson (e-mail), February 16, 2022–April 27,
    2022

Ralph O'Hara, December 10, 1995

Bob Phillips, August 26, 1995

Dora Reisser (e-mail), December 12, 2021–March 15, 2022

Norm Richards (e-mail), February–March 2016

Cheyney Ryan (e-mail), January 19, 2012

Lisa Ryan, December 16, 2011

Ed Silver, January 16, 2012

Elliot Silverstein, February 23, 1998

Donald Sutherland (e-mail), April 13, 2022, and April 27, 2022

Clint Walker, April 6, 1999, and December 9, 2016

Valerie Walker, March 7, 2022

Paul Wasserman, March 13, 1996

MISCELLANEOUS

Charles Bronson and Lee Marvin's military service records, via Norm Richards through the Freedom of Information Act

Regular updates via *Daily Variety*, *Weekly Variety*, and the *Hollywood Reporter*

INDEX

ABOUT THE AUTHOR

Dwayne Epstein was born in New York's Coney Island in
1960 and moved west with his family at age eight, spending the rest of his childhood in Cerritos, California. He moved
back east to attend Mercer Community College in New Jersey,
and served as an assistant editor for the five area newspapers of
Cranbury Publications. Early in his career, Epstein earned his
first professional writing credit reviewing films for Hearst Community Newspapers. He was the managing editor at Miller
Educational Materials, overseeing the publication of titles and
catalogs for three companies, and authoring several titles himself.

Epstein is the author of a number of young-adult biographies covering such celebrity personalities as Adam Sandler,
Will Ferrell, Hilary Swank, Nancy Pelosi, Hillary Clinton,
and Denzel Washington for Lucent Books' *People in the News*
series. For the company's *History Makers* series, he authored
Lawmen of the West. Epstein also contributed to Bill Krohn's
bestselling books *Hitchcock at Work* and *Joe Dante and the Gremlins of Hollywood*.

Prior to writing biographies, Epstein contributed to film
chronicles on a regular basis. He wrote for *Filmfax Magazine*
on subjects such as Bobby Darin, the Rat Pack, television pioneer Steve Allen, film director Sam Fuller, comic book artist
Neal Adams, *Invasion of the Body Snatchers* (1956) star Kevin
McCarthy, John Belushi, comedy legend Sid Caesar, actor
Clint Walker, and renowned graphic artist Greg Hildebrandt.

Epstein later contributed to *Cahiers du Cinema*'s "Serious Pleasures," which had a high profile in Europe. He wrote on American films chosen for rediscovery by directors Oliver Stone, Francis Ford Coppola, Woody Allen, and Clint Eastwood.

While working as an assistant editor on the *Jewish Community News*, Epstein's exclusive on the vandalizing of a temple in Long Beach, California, resulted in the perpetrators being prosecuted for a hate crime. In 2013 his biography *Lee Marvin: Point Blank* made the *New York Times* bestseller list at number four and garnered several publishing awards. He has also written several original articles for Emmy.com, including an examination of Lee Marvin's TV career and interviews with actor and comedian Nick Rutherford, actress Vella Lovell, and actress Seana Kofoed.

Epstein currently resides in Long Beach, California, with his girlfriend, Barbara. When he isn't writing, he enjoys watching and reading about movies and collecting soundtracks.